D1114634

WAITER, THERE'S A HORSE IN MY WINE

WAITER,
THERE'S A HORSE
IN MY WINE

A Treasury of Entertainment,
Exploration and Education
by America's Wittiest Wine Critic

Jennifer "Chotzi" Rosen

Dauphin Press
Denver, Colorado

First printing 2005
Printed in the United States of America

ISBN 0-9763170-0-1
Library of Congress Control Number: 2004098619

ATTENTION CORPORATIONS, UNIVERSITIES, COLLEGES, AND PROFESSIONAL ORGANIZAATIONS; Quantity discounts are available on bulk purchases of this book for educational, gift purposes, or as premiums for increasing magazine subscriptions or renewals. Special books or book excerpts can also be created to fit specific needs. For information, please contact Dauphin Press, 245 S Garfield St, Denver, CO 80209; 303-321-0211.

Illustrations by Gary Hovland
Interior design & typesetting by Lead Dog Communications; 720-344-8605

Contents

Part II: Wines

WHITE

RED

SPARKLING AND SWEET

Part III: Around the Globe

OLD WORLD

NEW WORLD

Part IV: Drinking and Tasting

USING YOUR SENSES

GOOD & BAD

RESTAURANT ISSUES

SERVING & DRINKING

Foreword

By Donald J.P. Ziraldo
President, Inniskillin Wines, Canada
Founding Chairman, Vintners Quality Alliance

If an award were to be given to the most irreverent wine writer, Jennifer Rosen would certainly qualify.

She writes with great wit, a sophisticated palate and a depth of knowledge which makes the story of wine compelling and, most importantly, fun.

The wine business is a very serious one and often, to the novice, creates a barrier to entry.

Jennifer's style not only compels the reader to look at wine in a whole new light but it pokes fun at some of the traditions and norms that have always perplexed wine drinkers:

On French winemakers: "They like women. They're fascinated by women. They cannot talk wine except in feminine terms."

On wine snobs: "I'm pretty good friends with Hamilton McFudders...the reclusive Napa producer of the legendary

Fudd's Vineyard Red, the only wine ever to receive a 101-point rating."

On labels: "If you've got some time, say, five years, I'll explain all about reading wine labels. Ten, if you want Germany."

She provides the reader with solid science, but makes it fun:

On corked wines: "Be honest: have you ever choked down weird wine in silence, thinking, perhaps, it was an acquired taste? I did, until I twigged to TCA...a chemical compound you can detect in concentrations akin to one sugar cube dissolved in 100 Olympic swimming pools."

On tannin: "Many people don't like vegetables, and the feeling is mutual. Tannin is the nightclub bouncer of the vegetable world."

On varietals with common names: "Pinot. The word keeps popping up like Paris Hilton in your spam box. Pinot Noir, Pinot Blanc, Pinot Grigio. What's up with that?"

It's easy to read these short, concise pieces and absorb the knowledge included.

This collection of columns provokes questions, answers detailed nuances and, most importantly, adds a sense of humor to the very intense, enjoyable art of wine.

Acknowledgments

So many people have made my wine life joyful and helped make this book possible. My deepest thanks to:

My first editor Bob Sweeney, who changed my life by making me shut up and start writing. Rocky Mountain News editors Maria Cote and Jay Dedrick, who fight off persnickety copy editors who want to "fix" my jokes, and maintain a relaxed attitude toward the concept of "deadline." Wine Enthusiast editor Tim Moriarty, who plucked me from cyberspace to put me in his pages.

Thanks to Jean-Noël Fourmeaux, for love, inspiration and always being available to talk me down off a ledge. To my ex-husband Mike Rosen, for his help and support, his healthy respect for nepotism, and for introducing me to the Laffer curve. To my father Blair Chotzinoff, who reads every column and whose encouragement means everything.

Thanks to Gary Hovland for his magnificent illustrations, and for being even a greater procrastinator than me. To Ann Alden for designing a kick-ass web page and graphics. To

Marina Chotzinoff, my sister and webmaster, who drags me kicking and screaming into her wonderful visions, inexplicably never gets annoyed, and sometimes works for wine.

Thanks to the UPS and Fed-Ex delivery guys for waking me up each morning so I get some work done. To Angela Hoxsey, for putting all the accents, umlauts and appellations in the right places. To Marilyn Ross for helping me make sense of the whole project.

Thanks to all the people and organizations that send me around the world, including Billington Imports, Wein aus Österreich, Deutsches Weininstitut, Thompson International Marketing and Appellation Imports.

And especially, thanks to all the readers who e-mail: I save your letters and turn to them whenever I begin to suspect my writing might be as bad as it really seems.

Introduction

You're baffled. You're not a wine idiot—you read up when you have the time and you've drunk a decent bottle or two. Yet your stomach dives when the sommelier hovers into view. He's sure to make hash of your shaky knowledge and expose you to the world (or at least to your table) as a phony.

You've frozen solid in the liquor store, paralyzed by shelf after endless shelf of Chardonnay. Your brain springs a leak; everything you know about wine trickles out. You leave, clutching a bottle you chose purely for the pretty sailboat on the label.

It's not like this buying cheese, or tires. You know what you know and you ask what you don't. There's got to be a key; a magic document, jealously guarded by a cabal of the wine-savvy. The *Rules*! If you could only find them, you'd never look stupid again!!

Guess what? I study wine all day, and have the same problem. I've had it since the age of ten, when I fell, and hard, for a bottle of Lancers Rosé. The sweet, pink fizz in the crockery

"You've frozen solid in the liquor store, paralyzed by shelf after endless shelf of Chardonnay."

bottle enchanted me. So did the gentle buzz and the way it made grownups inexplicably let me stay up later.

When I got older, I studied wine, collecting appellations and vintages like baseball statistics. If I couldn't actually afford the wines, at least I could chant the magic syllables: Vouvray, Volnay, Viognier, Vins de Pays...

I became a geek, who would pontificate at the drop of a hat. Eventually, a man turned to me and asked if I wouldn't shut up and write a weekly column for his newspaper, instead. I accepted, planning to explain The Rules. To arm the world! To make everyone suave and confident.

But a strange thing happened. The more I learned, the more I realized I didn't know. There is more fabulous wine available from every corner of the globe right now than ever before in history. Not a day goes by without someone saying, "Of course you know my favorite winery in Chile (or Australia, or Austria, or Sicily), Domaine Murray?" And I have to admit that, no, I don't. Even if Murray's Meritage did get 93 points from the Wine Emasculator.

If I can't keep up, how can you? Forget mastery. I know Master Sommeliers and Masters of Wine. These people are walking encyclopedias who can tell you the average rainfall in the Stellenbosch in August, 1996. Yet they, too, sometimes order clunkers at restaurants, or nod "OK" to wine that's clearly corked.

Forget money. While you fill your cellar with cases of highly-rated Bordeaux and Burgundy you're missing the extraordinary, value-priced stuff coming out of New Zealand and Sicily.

The key to loving wine without being hurt is humility. It's like parenting a teenager. You remember a solid little arm-bundle with rosy cheeks, a big smile and shining report cards.

Then along comes this hulking, pizza-faced creep, claiming you're related and embarrassing you in front of your friends. When you order a wine that once brought you joy and it arrives with a tongue ring and orange Mohawk—well, you can freak out, or, as my no-longer-teenage son suggests—you can chill.

Another way of saying, "Accept the process," a concept drilled into me by my college art professor. I'd be roaring in frustration, trying to draw with this crude bamboo pen he'd forced on me in place of a nice, obedient conte crayon, dripping blobs of ink all over my paper, and he'd say: "Accept the process. Don't fight the medium, embrace it. Flow with the inkiness. Let the ink-blot be the roundness of the model's breast."

And so it is with wine. Offer up your ignorance to the world like it was your virginity, celebrating, rather than hiding it. Dare to experiment, to ask questions and to embrace wine as a process of lifelong learning. Expect each bottle to be both a pleasure and a lesson (even when that lesson is "Never, ever order Latvian Verktvine again"). Then you can stop fearing wine and get on with the business of loving it.

Alas, I have no rules to give you. Only what I hope are memorable lessons, steps along a road, each to be savored as a singular experience. I hope they imbue you with some of my love and enthusiasm for the inscrutable, frustrating, sensual, gorgeous thing that is wine.

Part I: Preliminaries

VINEYARD

Western Civ 101

How wine saved history

Jesus was not a party animal. The Last Supper was hardly the blowout of the season. So why would he waste his quota of miracles on such frivolity as turning water into wine?

We use wine to celebrate, relax, pontificate and get drunk. It's hard to imagine that this frill on the apron of life was largely responsible for the rise of Western Civilization.

I'm exaggerating, right? You decide. The first Neolithic spree was probably honey gone bad. It's a short step from there to grapes. With their high sugar content and crushability, they practically vinify themselves. And you could always follow drunken bears into the woods to find where the grapes were fermenting.

But vines stripped in the course of a bison hunt make a short and awkward vintage. There's evidence to suggest that the transition from spear to John Deere owed more to the lure of the grape harvest then the thrill of the pigsty.

The move to agriculture brought food surpluses which begat cities and cuneiform and…sewage. So many people, so little water. Given the difficulties of delivering virgin spring water to a megalopolis, and since any running water around doubled as a bathroom, wine, for millennia, was the only safe thing to drink.

What would your life be like if your first cup in the morning were not a double low-fat latté, but a Cabernet? It would be a drunken fog, that's what. Virtually every invention of Western society, up until the 1600s, when coffee, tea and hot chocolate got people boiling water, was made by someone half-crocked. Now, it's not as bad as it sounds. Wine, at that point, had about a quarter the alcohol of your average California Zinfandel. It was also sweet, sour and pretty awful. You can imagine how bad, if they added seawater, lead and tree sap to make it taste better.

But even at minimal alcohol levels, it got some people drunk; especially women who tended to get all lascivious and dangerous. Where there is wine, there have always been spoilsports. Preach as they might, though, prohibitionists had no alternative to offer. Considering the rate of dysentery, cholera and typhoid in countries that still don't have safe water supplies today; you can only conclude that anti-wine activists throughout the ages must have been carted off by those diseases even as they preached temperance.

But wine was more than a life preserver, it was a life giver; a valuable source of calories, vitamins and minerals. Centuries of literature observing this invigorating property are not just poetic hogwash. If wine does not make us noticeably healthier now, it's because we're already too healthy to notice. Wine-drinking societies, more vigorous than abstemious ones, had a better shot at survival. Chances are you're descended from one.

Although we classify it, now, as a depressant, because its kick deserts you somewhere in the night, through much of history wine was the only mood lifter available. An oasis, for some, in a desert of drudgery. In the West, where they had not yet discovered the wonders of opium, much less ibuprofen, it was as close to anesthesia as you could get. For these reasons, wine has been classified as both food and powerful medicine, from Hippocrates and the Medical School at Alexandria, until up to a century ago.

Can you imagine a world where wine was fed to slaves to make them stronger? Or where the prospect of troops with no wine in their bellies made kings certain of defeat?

It's a minefield of paradoxes: Opus One-expensive and Thunderbird-cheap. Blood of Christ and work of Satan. For the rich and powerful and for guys who sleep under bridges. Gentrified pastime and threat to society. And now you know: builder of empires.

Heat Wave

Is global warming changing wine?

Global warming, they say, is affecting wine. For the first time in a millennium the phrase "English Wine" does not require a smirk. Germany is producing drinkable reds, a move every bit as surprising as if they swapped "Achtung" for "Aloha" and turned their beer halls into Tiki rooms.

Recent studies claim that fifty years of warming have improved wine and will continue to do so. On the other hand, vin- and viticulture have progressed so astronomically during the same period that you can't arbitrarily credit the weather.

Not every region is sweating. For each sweltering summer, like this last in Europe, another region, like Niagara, reported its coldest, rainiest season yet. So should we be looking forward to wine-in-a-bagpipe, or at least more concentrated Bordeaux? Sidestep the question of planetary tilt vs. hairspray and carburetors, and you can't deny major climate change as far back as our ice-core sampling equipment can reach.

The last time British wines held sway was the Medieval Warm Period, a weird heat spike beginning around 900 A.D.. It lasted only 400 years, but that was long enough for the Western World to explode with crops, children, exploration and cathedrals, not to mention clearing the icebergs for Leif Erikson to stumble upon America.

Then the Little Ice Age crept slowly in and hung around until the 19th century. No one wanted to believe it. Crops failed on Greenland and Iceland and residents had to beat their plowshares into harpoons. There was starvation, death, and bubonic plague. Orange groves froze in China. The population plummeted. People skated on the Thames.

Like a tide, the climate sweeps in and out, depositing a population here, wiping out another over there. When it's hot, excess people swarm north, looking for new land to conquer. When it's cold they swarm south, looking for countries to invade. (People in the southern hemisphere do the same thing upside down.)

In the face of all that life and death, the minutia of wine connoisseurship seems a little silly. Too much acid, too much sugar—for God's sake! a few degrees colder and we wouldn't have the luxury of complaining about flabby Chardonnay. Those freezing, starving Greenlanders would say, "Flab? Where? Give me some!!"

Yet tiny wine/weather changes produce huge cultural ones. If a wine district has three great vintages in a decade, it's a star. Growers flock to get a piece of the glory, dismissing the seven mediocre years as a fluke. If a region should experience three *dreadful* years in ten, though, put a fork in it.

The search for balanced Claret might seem a frivolous one, but it makes waves. England's thirst drove her to France, Spain and Portugal, leading to marriages, wars and alliances: a bigger effect on history, arguably, than the Vikings settling and abandoning Newfoundland.

Climate change will happen. Whether it's positive—say the ice caps melt and inundate New York—or negative, like the nightmare scenario envisaged by Loire Valley winemaker Jean-Luc Soty of Pascal Jolivet in which, "Changes in the fruit may result in a Sancerre that is not, perhaps, what one expects of a Sauvignon!"

If Italy and Spain get too hot for Garnacha, Denmark will take up the slack. A shame, perhaps, to lose all those centuries of Burgundian know-how. But the French will adapt in their usual, accommodating way.

It's a winner for consumers. We need only reach out and grab good wine as the climate rolls around. We can discover treasure in emerging regions. My hunch is they wouldn't have emerged in an ice age. As Thorfinn Karlsefni said in 1071, describing the last vintage on Newfoundland, "A bountiful harvest indeed and undoubtedly many more to come!"

A Very Good Year

Do vintages matter?

The year 121 B.C., according to Roman historian Pliny the Elder, was "a vintage of the highest excellence." He wrote that in 70 A.D., nearly 200 years later, so chances are he was bluffing, as wine writers do. In any case, it didn't impress his brother, Pliny the Welder, who preferred beer. You've heard people gush about an '82 Bordeaux or a '63 port, but why do vintages differ, and are they really important enough to pay attention to?

Years are important simply because grapes are important. No matter how talented the winemaker, Hungarian-oak-barrel-stave-inserts notwithstanding, he's only as good as the grapes he's working with. Among agricultural products, grapes have an odd temperament; they thrive, like a Jewish mother, on suffering. Forget Miracle Gro. Poor, rocky soil; lousy irrigation; gnarled, stunted vines; ripped-off leaves; these produce grapes that may grow up to be an expensive bottle of wine some day.

"The year 121 B.C., according to Roman historian Pliny the Elder, was a vintage of the highest excellence. This didn't impress his brother, Pliny the Welder, who preferred beer."

There's a fine line between nurturing and killing a grape vine. Spring frost can zap new buds. Frying summer makes "flabby" wine, that is, high on sugar, low on flavor and zing. Harvest time is a real nail-biter. Pick too early and the wine tastes unripe or "green." Wait a day longer and it might rain, filling the grapes with water and diluting a summer's worth of complexity.

Some wines don't even exist except in freak years. Germany's Trockenbeerenauslese (go ahead, try it; no one's listening) depends on grapes left hanging on the vine into December, which seldom works. The so-called "noble rot," which produces ethereal dessert wines in Sauternes, only deigns to arrive when the weather is just so.

In Portugal and Champagne, the growing conditions from year to year are so important that a vintage isn't even "declared" unless it's considered exceptional. That means if the wine's not good enough, they blend it with others and don't list a year on the bottle.

Can you memorize a couple of magic numbers that will guarantee you wonderful wine every time? Sorry, it's not that easy. Even in a great year, some wineries miss out. On the bright side, in dreadful years a few lucky wineries manage to make decent stuff, which can be a fantastic bargain if you know what to look for.

Also, climates differ all over the world, so a great year in Italy is not necessarily a great one in Australia. Weather is remarkably unreliable in Europe, so the difference between a good and bad year there is profound. We're much luckier here. The weather doesn't have dramatic variations in California, so while great years are great, bad years are pretty good, too.

If money's no object, should you always steer towards the "classic" years? Not really. Often a spectacular vintage means an age-worthy wine. But these can be as tough as an old boot when they're young. If you're buying for your cellar, by all means go for the best years, but if you're planning on drinking now, "ready" trumps "great."

If you enjoyed memorizing the periodic table of the elements in high school, you can skip this part. For the rest of us, there are vintage charts: nifty devices that rate years by country and type of wine, and advise whether to drink now, or hold for later. A generalization, yes, but a handy one. If you don't care to get into this kind of detail, though, don't worry. Chances are, thanks to modern weather forecasting, neither grapes nor you will get burned.

Trial by Terroir

The voice of the vineyard

The difference between Old- and New-World wines is embodied neatly in the fact that there is no French word for "winemaker," and no American word for *terroir*. In France, you produce wine the way you raise children; shepherd them through their vulnerable years, protect them from their own stupidity and try to instill some values. Fully expect each kid to have his own personality, and when he comes home with orange hair and a little silver barbell in his eyebrow let him know he's still part of the fold. If you did your job right, the family values are lurking just under the surface and will emerge as soon as he starts to pay his own income taxes.

To drag this metaphor kicking and screaming into the vineyard, the point is that the French producer is a *vigneron*, not winemaker. That is, he raises grapes, and it's up to the grapes to decide what sort of wine they want to be when they grow up.

In the end, the grape never falls far from the vine. This inevitable family imprint, when applied to wine, is known as *terroir*; a combination of soil, temperature, rainfall and sunlight that's much more than the sum of its parts.

As Americans, we instinctively resist this tyranny of nature over science. This is the land of Rogaine and Viagra, for heaven's sake! Surely, the sophisticated winemaker knows enough alchemy to spin mediocre grapes into gold!

Grapes, however, are old fashioned. Raising geraniums is simple by contrast: you water, weed, fertilize and are rewarded with nice big flowers. Vigorous, bushy grapevines, however, do not make for good wine. Even big, plump, juicy grapes don't guarantee it. The formula for stellar wine grapes is much more elusive.

Moreover, the damned things are ungrateful. Masochists, actually. Not for them, the rich, vibrant loam of the New World. They like their soil lunar, stripped and rocky. They prefer to fight for every ounce of water they get, sending roots down as far as twenty-five feet to lick up a few tiny drops. Don't blame them. Blame the ancient Romans.

Back in the good old days, when a guy didn't need a frat party to go around in a toga, the Romans had a habit of up and invading Europe whenever there wasn't much else to do. First order of business when conquering your neighbor is to insure yourself a supply of food and drink. So Romans would set about planting grain in the fertile valleys, and grapes on the craggy hillsides where nothing else would grow.

As a result, all over Europe you still see vines clinging to barren slopes steep enough to induce vertigo in a funicular goat. Grapes slowly adapted themselves to this privation, as well as to the tastes of local drinkers. Countless random experiments gradually determined the best of all possible places for each variety to shine.

The phenomenon that Burgundy, the place, and Pinot Noir, the grape, seem to be made for each other, is no accident. They literally were. It's a matter of optimal *terroir*.

Fast-forward a few thousand years to California in the early days of the grape rush. Speculators arrive—grape vine in hand—ready to create their own little slice of vineyard heaven. Where to begin? Do you plant what you drank in the old country? Do you grow Cabernet, because, damn it, you've just always had a yen to make Cabernet? Do you make like a pioneer and try a little of everything? Growers tried all these approaches and more. But the grape continued to call the shots.

In the end, it brought even the can-do, Yankee winemaker to his knees. The smart ones have thrown in the white flag or raised the towel or whatever you do to surrender and conceded that without *terroir*—that is, an excellent site married to the perfect grape—they'd never make better than mediocre wine.

Understandably, the few magic spots on earth where wine grapes transcend the ordinary and trend towards the sublime are valuable real estate. The brave winemakers who resist the temptation to meddle too much, standing back instead and letting the grapes strut their stuff, take risks that standardized, homogenous wineries avoid. Because it's rare and expensive to make, this sort of wine doesn't sell for ten dollars at the grocery store.

But the taste and smell of first class *terroir*, be it Napa or Alsace, Burgundy or Bordeaux, kind of spoils you for supermarket wine, anyway. France and America both have plenty of words for it: *Extraordinaire! Formidable!* Heavenly! Delicious!

Stop the Cruelty!

Torturing vines for better grapes

I'm writing on behalf of the Society for the Prevention of Cruelty to Grapes (SPCG) and Girls Against Grape Abuse (GAGA). I'm fed up with the terrible things that are done in the name of wine. Across the globe, vines are being tortured, violently de-foliated, starved for water and nutrients and made to grow in inhospitable places. As you read this sentence, one million vines will be bound by their canes to trellises, forced to assume humiliating and unnatural positions. Something must be done!

Vinous abuse, the silent tragedy, is hardly new. Early Europeans, and the invaders who raped and pillaged them, were kind to other crops. They planted grain in fertile valleys, watering it, even pampering it. But life was always different for grapevines. They were and are routinely relegated to barren backwaters where nothing else will grow: Hillsides so steep you need pitons and carabiners to harvest. Desolate cliffs buffeted by chilling winds. Vineyards, in Châteauneuf-du-Pape for instance, with fist-sized rocks where soil should be. Wastelands in Portugal where planting-holes are blasted out of granite with dynamite.

Any stray scraps of nutrient that vines might have turned to for comfort were long ago stripped away by eons of farming. To survive in these hostile conditions, grapes were forced to assimilate; leaving their own diverse cultures and habits behind. Only the shrewd ones made it; operators who knew how to charm a local yeast.

For a while, the New World, with its teaming topsoil and virgin-forest mulch, held out the promise of a life of ease and respect. Alas, in short order the species was subjugated there as before; made to feel like a second-class vegetable.

How does man justify its inhumanity to grapes? A spare-the-rod ethos is often invoked: privation is necessary, the theory goes, to instill a work ethic in your children when you've got a Humvee parked in the garage. Lazy leaves that don't shoulder their share of the photosynthesis burden must be ripped off, leaving endless toil to the few that remain. Vines are often crowded together—sometimes less than a meter apart—and then forced, by extreme pruning and head training, to grovel so they don't shade each other from the sun.

I witnessed a poignant sight in Burgundy: a section of hillside sliced open for construction, laying bare the very personal, underground life of a vineyard for prurient eyes to ogle as though it were a child's ant-farm. This intimate view revealed roots growing thirty feet down through strata of stone, in a heartbreaking search for water. Winemakers condone this practice, citing the mineral flavors that come from the soil, but the truth is much, much worse.

These are vines in emergency mode, face to face with their own, almost certain death. Martyrs to the survival of their very species, they prepare by taking all their assets out of such peripherals as roots, leaves and stems and investing them in fruit. With all their remaining strength, they generate dark, sweet, luscious berries, the kind that catch the attention of birds and bears and wild boars in the fervent hope that these animals will eat the fruit and then transport it with them to a better, gentler world. There, the undigested seeds, wrapped in neat packages of fertilizer, could nestle in and start a new life, filled with new hope. Do we let this happen? No. In a final orgy of cruelty, we pick the berries, crush them and make them wine.

Are you going to stand by and let this happen? I call upon each and every one of you to join with me in stopping the insanity! Grapes have feelings, too! Oh, wait a minute, no they don't. Never mind.

WINERY

Ode to Ethyl

Can we talk about alcohol?

Oceans of ink describe the aroma, flavor and color in wine, but you seldom hear much about alcohol. It's almost bad taste to admit you're aware of it, let alone praise it. Yet it's tremendously responsible for all that's good in wine.

Beyond the way it makes you happy, beyond its propensity to unlace inhibitions and leave your judgment so wrapped around the axel that you wake up with your arm trapped under a disturbingly canine person of the opposite sex, beyond the buzz, lie respectable reasons to appreciate alcohol.

"Nuances of ripe, Asian moonfruit" would not exist without alcohol to transport their odors and flavors. When you swirl—"volatize the esters," to be crude—alcohol carries these components up the sides of the glass and then evaporates, leaving them clinging there for you to smell. De-alcoholized wine shows none of these subtleties. Or maybe it's just that sober people don't write like that.

A solvent, alcohol extracts tannin and color from grapes. Thank it, too, for body; the sensuous, oily texture also known as mouth-feel. Oddly, for an odorless and tasteless substance, it also makes dry wine taste a little sweet.

Hard to believe alcohol makes wine rich, sweet and smooth, considering what it feels like on an open wound. But it only starts burning when there's way too much of it. Too little, and the wine ends up watery and insipid. What would Goldilocks do?

She'd look for balance. If fruit, acid, tannin, sugar and alcohol all sing together in harmony, none of them sticking out like Julie Frumquit in your high school choir, then you've got balanced wine. Enough fruit can hide a hefty dose of alcohol. Dessert wines are usually very alcoholic; the sugar keeps your palate from caring.

Have you ever wondered how Europeans drink wine at lunch without zonking out back at the office? Their wine has less alcohol than ours. This is not an evil plot, hatched in the cabals of globalization. It's simply that sugar ferments into alcohol and sun is what coaxes grapes to make sugar. Too much sun is not Europe's problem, quite the inverse. Some areas require minimum alcohol levels; you can't go much lower than the eight percent in some German Riesling. Old World winemakers sometimes resort to adding sugar to boost alcohol levels, a quasi-illegal practice known as *chaptalization*.

New World wine regions, especially Australia and California, have the opposite problem: intense sun crams grapes full of sugar before they've developed much flavor. Blockbuster Zinfandel and Syrah can rise as high as fifteen percent, even sixteen percent alcohol. Without masses of fruit, it can be undrinkable. In this case, serving at cooler temperatures goes a long way to calming the towering-inferno effect.

Enormous wines can be luscious—don't forget the body, sweetness and flavor we discussed above. But when it comes to washing down food, they're about as refreshing as hot chocolate or Pepto Bismol. The real rip-off comes when you can only drink half as much of them, or find yourself exploring the under-table world of the vessel Collapso.

European wines, though, are getting hotter. The sun hasn't turned up a notch, but weather prediction has. Harvest time always meant weighing the benefit of ripe grapes against the risk of rain, wind and storms. Modern meteorology has made it safe to leave grapes hanging longer, building up more flavor, along with more sugar to ferment into alcohol.

Next wine you drink, consider checking the alcohol percentage. It's required on all American labels, with a variance of plus or minus a percent and a half.

After years of being blamed for the sins of the world, isn't it time this poor, misunderstood substance was given a little respect? Speak proudly of the alcohol in your wine, at least if you're going to yammer on about hints of Swedish raffia in a finberry emulsion.

The Wild, Wild Yeast

And winemakers who wrangle it

"Winemaker" is kind of a misnomer for a human. The title *should* belong to the single-celled fungi who really make the wine: yeast.

The human's job, besides being chemist, artist and farmer, is to ride herd on these guys. You don't just flip a switch on the Wine-O-Matic and watch them work. They must be selected, introduced to their job, fed, nurtured, and persuaded to die at the appropriate time. The yeast-wrangler also breaks up fights and cleans up after the critters. He has to stay sharp, because, like wire clothes hangers, these little catalysts can double their population in two hours. It's not unusual to find five million in one drop of fermenting wine.

They pay their own board in the end, by performing the miracle of fermentation: turning glucose into alcohol. Despite many delightful stories about the discovery of wine, it was surely happening on its own for millennia, long before man got into the act, since sugary things like grapes ferment easily, and grape skins swarm with wild yeast.

But wild is not always the best kind for the job. Some can't take the heat, literally, that the fermentation process gives off, dying before their work is done. Others can't hold their liquor, and quit when the alcohol level gets too high. Both scenarios leave sugar in wine; a dangerous situation. A gang of outlaw yeast could start that sugar fermenting again in the bottle, where you can't control them. If you want to make a wine with some sweetness, you need to run every one of them doggies out of Dodge by filtering assiduously before you bottle.

Modern winemakers skirt some of these problems by inoculating the grape juice with domestic yeast. They have a large catalog to choose from. Some yeasts are hell-raisers, snorting and pitching up bubbles like a volcano. OK in an open tank, but not so smart when you're working with a small oak barrel. Others specialize in different types of fermentation, for instance, the secondary one that puts bubbles in Champagne.

Different yeasts frame and emphasize different flavors and odors. One might bring out butterscotch, cream and hazelnut in a white. Another could highlight jammy and cedar notes in a red, or promote a long, licorice finish. Some take the edge off acidity, while others punch up color.

When fermenting is through, and the little guys have gone to that great feedlot in the sky, their remains sink slowly to the bottom of the barrel. But their work is not over. They are now known as "lees," and the wrangler can choose to leave the wine on them—or *sur lies*—for months, or siphon it into a clean barrel, a process known as *racking*. Longer lees time usually results in thicker, more viscous mouth-feel in the finished wine.

What did they do before modern yeast-busting? For centuries, winemakers returned the mass of pressed-out grape-skins to the vineyards as fertilizer. Called *pumice*, it was filled with yeast, specifically the particular yeast that had dominated the fermentation. It would then proceed to dominate the vineyard. Gradually, this changed the local types of yeast until each area developed its own selected strain. By simply encouraging spontaneous fermentation, winemakers could get pretty predictable results. But when starting a vineyard in, say, California, it's more convenient not to wait 500 years for the right yeast strains to select themselves, so we turn to the lab.

The next time you notice a toastiness, a baking-bread aroma in your glass of Champagne, stop and think for a moment of the brave men and women who regularly put their livelihood on the line, taming yeast.

Over a Barrel

The use (and misuse) of oak

Scene 1: A man stands on an empty stage, strumming a guitar and singing a simple, haunting song. Add a touch of bass and drums. Give the guy a microphone, just enough to project the nuances of his voice. Weave in a little violin; sweet, but not schmaltzy.

Scene 2: A pretty teenager, with a voice as flat as her belly and as airy as her brain, sings a repetitive song with scant melody, and lyrics that define banality. Add a window-shattering beat, turn up the reverb and plaster on layers of synthesized instrumentals. Bring in a choreographer and ten backup dancers, add a smoke machine and strobe lights, and shoot a video.

You're getting an idea of the different roles of oak in wine.

Once just a storage vessel, oak has become one of the most important tools in the wine-maker's arsenal, and one of the most contested. When wine is fermented or aged in small oak barrels, it absorbs a lot of wood character.

31

"Oak barrels are expensive so these wines cost more."

What's so tasty about lumber? At its best, oak is the music producer in Scene 1. Its job is to frame and polish. It rounds out flavors and pumps up body. It smoothes minor flaws and adds complex nuances of its own.

Winemakers fine-tune their woodwork, seeking a balance of old wood, which is neutral, and new wood, which is strong. They choose their forests, as the differences between American, French and Hungarian wood are profound. They decide how they want their barrels toasted, a process that caramelizes starch, and brings out traces of vanillin, resulting in flavors as varied as almonds, mint, coconut and coffee.

Oak tannins even have the power to erect and sensitize your taste buds. (Don't get any ideas.) But unless you're in the business of discerning organoleptic components, ideally you don't *taste* oak at all.

Flying winemaker Michel Roland says there are no over-oaked wines, only under-fruited ones. Welcome to the flipside: underwhelming wines, tweaked out of recognition by oak extract and giant tea bags filled with oak chips, in short, the barrel equivalent of an MTV production crew. If oak is an amplifier, this sort of wine is turned up to eleven.

It's what Europe thinks America likes—a bland McWine, bereft of subtlety. True, it sells very well. Are we a bunch of insensitive idiots? Nah, it's just that there's too damn much wine out there. We don't know where to start. So we look for assurance from reviewers who routinely judge fifty samples or more in one sitting. Predictably, the brassier wines stand out like Ethel Merman in a Trappist monastery. Oak garners ratings.

Oak barrels are expensive and need to be replaced often, so these wines cost more. The overwhelmed wine consumer, seeking guidance, sees what looks like a solid plank to cling to: high ratings plus high price must equal better wine. Ergo, the taste of oak equals the taste of quality.

Europe, however, underestimates us. The "American Taste" label they love to slap on us doesn't stick. We're a nation of individuals with unpredictable desires. And if we have one thing in common, it's that we're open to change.

There's been a shootout at the oak-ay corral. Americans are discovering the surprising freshness and food-friendliness of un-oaked and less-oaked wine. The axiom "great wine is made in the vineyard" finally makes sense.

Wine, like a beautiful voice, should sometimes be left alone to express itself.

If Tannins Could Talk

They'd say "Don't eat me!"

More and more I read about wines having "sweet tannins," but no one can tell me what they are. I suspect über wine-authority Robert Parker of kick starting the term, but his explanation of it is vague. The whole thing is mystifying if you know much about tannins.

Many people don't like vegetables, and the feeling is mutual. Tannin is the nightclub bouncer of the vegetable world. It fends us off with its rough, astringent texture. It binds to saliva proteins and whisks them away, leaving your mouth feeling troweled in spackle. Then there's nothing for it but to re-lubricate with something fat, like a twelve-ounce rib-eye, which is why when a wine wrings out your tongue and hangs it up to dry, someone will invariably say, "But it's a FOOD wine." (What it's not, is a *dry* wine. Dry, in wine parlance, refers to lack of sweetness, not to texture.)

"Cows are no strangers to drunkenness. Four stomachs of fermenting grain can turn you into a walking Moo-'n-Brew."

The taste of tannin is bitter—like the papery skin of a walnut. But peoples' perception varies wildly. Sensitive palates sometimes find tannic bitterness drowning out every other taste, numbing them even to subsequent wines. Meanwhile, all around them, people are raving about lush fruit. But enough about Chile.

If you don't like red wine, it's probably the tannins. They come from the skins and seeds of the grape, which are separated from white wines very early in the winemaking process. Some tannin also comes from oak barrels, and a little—the practice is sort of hush-hush—is added by winemakers. Now, why would they want to go and do that?

Because tannin isn't all-bad. By inhibiting oxidation, it acts as a preservative. It's a must if wine is going to age long enough to develop complexity in the bottle. It has the decency to surrender in the end, so that a wine can be very drinkable at forty, even if it tasted like a Sahara sandwich at four.

It also adds structure. Up till now we've discussed *unripe* tannins. Fully ripe grapes, handled ever so gently, will also show *ripe* tannins. These have longer molecules, too big to fit into your tannin receptors, so instead of all that nastiness, you just get a sensation of body. Besides, a touch of the rough stuff acts like a pinch of salt, waking up soft wines that would otherwise sink into insipidity.

Why, in view of a yeoman's effort on the part of the plant kingdom, do we like wine? According to a study on cows, we're not just drawn to food by taste, but also by post-ingestive effects—i.e., how we feel afterwards. If you throw up after a clambake, you may never buy bi-valves again, even if stomach flu turns out to be the culprit. Cows have no palate for *serecia*, a tannic and toxic plant, unless it's dredged in polyethylene glycol, which happens to neutralize the plant's poison effects.

They don't know this consciously, but it's why they find the taste, or perhaps the buzz, of that chemical appealing. Cows are no strangers to drunkenness. Four stomachs full of fermenting grain can turn you into a walking Moo-'n-Brew.

We've learned recently that the anti-oxidant properties of tannin are good for us, but, ironically, vegetable growers have spent most of the last century breeding out the bitterness, and with it the anti-oxidants. They're not about to try turning the American public onto New, Extra-Bitter Broccoli! Perhaps one day they'll discover those elusive sweet tannins.

When Corks Attack

They do it with TCA

It was hardly an international incident, but embarrassing all the same. The highly touted Zinfandel I ordered to impress visiting winemaker Xavier Berger-Devieux, proprietor of Burgundy's Manoir de Mercey, wasn't really terrible, just...blah. I meant to show that America had the chops, vinously speaking, to give France a run for her Euros. But I blew it.

Or did I? Perhaps the wine was corked, or tainted by 2,4,6-Trichloroanisole (TCA), a chemical compound you can detect in concentrations akin to one sugar cube dissolved in 100 Olympic swimming pools.

Corked wines smell musty, grassy, reminiscent of wet cardboard. So if my Zinfandel was corked, wouldn't I know it? Not necessarily. TCA can also steal in, make off with all the fruit, aromas, and other goodies, and scamper out without leaving a trace. Monsieur Berger-Devieux was as flummoxed as I was. Check it out: two wine professionals, reduced to "Um, it shouldn't taste like this...should it?"

Kumeu River Winery in New Zealand rejected forty-two out of sixty-two batches of cork in 1998, but got contamination anyway. "Many customers did not identify cork taint, but just thought that the wine was perhaps not very good. We have no way of knowing how many customers were lost," they said.

Be honest: have you ever choked down weird wine in silence, thinking, perhaps, it was an acquired taste? I did, until I twigged to TCA. Now I can't avoid it. Corked bottles are running one for six in my tasting lab. When it happens—wham!—there goes the wine's chance for a recommendation. Too bad for them, at least I didn't pay for the bottle. How about when you do? "A $15 Pinot Blanc turns up corked, that's sad, but a $300 Romanée-Conti you've stored for ten years—that's tragedy," says Hubert Trimbach of Alsace. Even his ultra-reliable, eponymous winery has had cork issues.

The race is on to clean up corks. TCA gets an early start, in the forests. A close cousin, Tribromoanisol (TBA), lurks in flame-retardant chemicals and fungicides. Both settle into the wood and air of old wineries. With the tenacity of a packing peanut in a thunderstorm, they refuse to be evicted, thriving on the very boiling and chlorine that's used to dislodge them. Microwaves were tried, to little effect. New micro-organism-fighting enzymes have yet to prove their mettle.

Could they be fighting the wrong battle? What, after all, is the big hoo-ha about a cork? Tradition? Would the same nostalgia apply to prescription cough syrup sealed this way? Corks relegate wine to the crab-leg and artichoke ghetto—too labor-intensive for daily use. Personally, I prefer easy access. For me, uncorking has all the romance of stopping to put on a condom.

Call me bitter: in my job you pack a corkscrew and I've now surrendered twelve to airport security. It's not the screw that irks them, it's the toy knife attached. What becomes of confiscated corkscrews, I sometimes wonder. Do they melt them all down and make a spiral staircase?

Synthetic corks are just as inconvenient. Plus, they don't form a good seal with glass; eventually they leak, or imbue the wine with a plastic whiff of *Eau de Mattel*.

You've arrived at the climax of this polemic: a plea for screw-caps. Oh, fine for young wine, you think, but doesn't older wine require cork to develop? It's a living thing that needs to breathe, right? Wrong and wrong again. And did I mention wrong? Aging is a reductive process, no oxygen involved. The amount the cork lets in is negligible, anyway.

Study after study shows screw-capped wine having more fruit, less oxidation and less variability than wine in cork. It matures slowly and gracefully and, best of all, contains no TCA. So while you might complain about a corked wine now, you'll never have to send one back because it's screwed.

What will it take to win over skittish drinkers? A prize under the cap (Win a Trip to the Winery!)? The convenience of storing screw-capped bottles upright, like your normal stuff? One day, corkscrews will be a collector's curiosity, along with snuffboxes and chamber pots. Until then, see if you can learn what TCA smells like, if you don't know already. You've been warned: the next cork you meet could be a killer.

Screw Loose & Fancy Free

Bottles & boxes & cans, oh, my!

Messing around my wine cellar yesterday, it occurred to me what one rogue bowling ball could do to my bottles. How frail they are! While fabric softener and 10W40 follow their R&D into ever more sophisticated containers, we œnophiles stick with bottle and cork. The arrangement's been around only a few centuries, yet you'd think wine wasn't wine without it.

Fragile bottles aside, corks are trouble to remove and hardly worth putting back in again. They handle the job of sterile, hermetic sealing the way barrel staves handle a black diamond run. The medical industry upgraded decades ago, acknowledging corks were nothing but spongy resort-hotels for microbes.

If not corks, what? Screw tops lead the pack. They preserve, protect and re-seal beautifully. The wine elite and the paper-bag set accept them cheerfully. It's the mass of uncertain consumers in between who continue to be suspicious.

"You'll never have to send wine back because it's screwed."

There's buzz about another retro closure: the crown-top. Elegant word for bottle-cap; the old soda and beer top with the crimped sides. If you think it doesn't dignify wine, consider this: Champagne ages for four to seven years in a crown-top before being corked. But unless you have the front teeth of a chipmunk, you need a tool to get it off, and then there's no putting it back.

"Metacork" is a new capsule that lets you unscrew the cork and then reseal the bottle. It doesn't solve the problem of cork-taint, though. And virgin wine-waiters with stage fright notwithstanding, I think people LIKE corkscrews. Snuff boxes, cigar cutters, ball markers; any self-respecting vice has its equipment and rituals.

Google "Zork" (I didn't talk this way before the Martians came), and you get The Great Underground Empire, a fantasy game. A different Zork is about to storm the wine-closure market. It's a black plastic gadget that makes a safe seal, doesn't screw, requires no tool, and you can put it back on. Most important, it goes "Pop!" Apparently this is something consumers feel strongly about.

Meanwhile, re-calibrate your snob-o-meter to wine-in-a-box. It's hip to be square. Oh, I know, for years those quadrilateral quaffs were nothing but Chardonnay-flavored apple juice. That's not the box's fault. It's an excellent container. The plastic bladder inside collapses and keeps out air as you siphon wine from the spigot below. Opened boxes drink well for weeks. Premium wine from California and Australia is coming soon to a box near you.

Do you have Château Albert in a Can? You might, soon. Still and sparkling wines have arrived in pull-tab aluminum cans, coated inside to keep out contamination and metal flavors. Ideal for picnics, ballgames, planes and trains.

A team of British design students recently introduced the Self Cooling Animated Bottle (SCAB?) with a temperature control device and itsy-bitsy TV on the label which plays tiny videos about grapes, wine making, tasting notes and food matches.

At the other end of the spectrum, there are still country stores in Italy and France where you can fill your own jerry can with red or white from something that looks, my source says, "exactly like a gas pump, complete with the little numbers metering around." I think I'd prefer that to a bottle with a TV on it. In the end, though, it doesn't much matter what the wine arrives in, so long as it ends up in your glass.

LAW

Appellation Spring

Appellations: overlapped & understood

If you've got some time, say, five years, I'll explain all about reading wine labels. Ten, if you want Germany. Since the bottling statement alone—there's a difference between "made" "cellared," "grown," "produced," and "vinted"—will spin your head, today we'll just look at appellations.

To head the obligatory joke off at the pass, an appellation is NOT a guy with five teeth who plays the banjo. It's a legal statement about quality and where the grapes came from. It shouldn't be too difficult to explain just as soon as I finish this bottle of Valium.

In the New World, comprising Australia, South Africa and the Americas, appellations are purely geographical. But they are not laid out edge to edge like tiles on the kitchen floor. Imagine, instead, that you spill a cup of coffee on the floor, and then drop a bowl of cornflakes into and around the puddle. What have you got? Layers. *American Viticultural Area,* or AVA,

47

is the term for appellation in America. Let's say the whole floor represents the United States AVA. Each tile is *also* a state AVA. Within the California tile, the coffee splatters are *also* county AVAs. One of the cornflakes in the Sonoma County coffee spill is *also* the Alexander Valley AVA.

A winemaker in that cornflake could claim any one of those AVAs. But he'd choose Alexander Valley, because the more *specific* the appellation, the better (and often more expensive) the wine. A bottle from the "Pacific Northwest" generally delivers less than one from "Jean-Pierre's Half-Acre."

Jean-Pierre can plant Thomson Seedless, for all our government cares, but in Europe, appellations are strictly controlled for quality. In France, for instance, if you're lucky enough to make red wine in Burgundy's Côte d'Or (pronounced: coat door), the grape must be Pinot Noir. You may not irrigate, or produce more than three tons per acre. Your vines must be spaced exactly one meter apart in every direction and be no higher than three feet, and, as far as I can tell, your name must be Jean-Claude, Jean-Pierre, or Jean-Marie, which— I can't help it—always struck me as a silly name for a man.

Appellations in Burgundy are so convoluted and layered that even most Burgundians don't understand them, but they do ensure a certain level of quality.

An Italian label might list the place, the place plus the grape, the grape plus the place, or the place plus the wine style. If you don't know the names of the over-100 Italian wine grapes, I challenge you to even find the appellation.

In Germany, an appellation is a meld of region, vineyard, grape, and *quality level*, determined by the amount of sugar in the grapes.

Just when you start to get a handle on all this, along comes the European Union and slaps its own regulations on all the EU countries, trumping all the national labeling laws.

Why the big deal about where the damned grapes grew, anyway? Because certain minute areas of the globe produce grapes like no others. Ernst Loosen, who makes highly acclaimed Riesling from his family's estates in the Mosel and Pfalz, rants for hours about the strangling German government regulations that make doing business there a nightmare. So why doesn't he just up and move to a country that supports free enterprise? Because his handful of acres is pure gold.

At least European appellations have the decency to change at glacial speed, unlike in the New World where they're dividing like cells in a Petri dish. Australia is poised to expand its number of appellations ten-fold, and wineries are fighting tooth and nail to hang onto the prestigious ones, instead of being stuck with a new, untested name.

But where does this mess leave you, the label reader, the drinker? As a rule of thumb, go for the most specific appellation you can afford. If you discover a wine that really pops your cork, look for others from the same appellation. Oh, and clean up that kitchen floor.

Reserve Judgment

"Proprietor's Reserve Cellar Select" means...what?

Résumé writing, they say, is all about active verbs. A previous job where you "stapled," "folded," or "cowered," won't do at all. To get a foot in the door, you've got to report that you Circumnavigated! Defenestrated! Spearheaded! Corrupted! Paint yourself as someone who sweeps problems off the face of the earth and will do it again if they hire you.

Even if you spent the last ten years putting stickers on apples, the right words will make a player out of you. They do the same for wine. I'm proud to say I have a cellar full of Proprietor's Selection, Private Selection, Select Vineyards, Vintner's Collection, Coastal Reserve and Show Reserve. Whoop-de-do!

You can't begrudge the producers a little hyperbole. Competition on the wine shelves is fierce these days. The advantage goes to the bottle that waves its hand and shouts, "Hey, over here! Try me!!"

Some parts of the wine label are strictly regulated, including vintage year, type of grape and region of origin. Quality statements, however, are a free-for-all. They took off just after prohibition, when Beaulieu Vineyards released a Napa Valley Cabernet designated "Reserve." Inglenook jumped on the train with "Limited Cask." This eventually led to the gaggle of wines we see today, so private, select and reserved you'd think it was alumni week at Eton.

"Reserve," the most common enhancer, is usually a guarantee you'll pay more. But it's no predictor of quality. It's not unheard of for a Reserve bottle to score lower than its cheaper stable mate in a blind tasting. Even winemakers who honestly respect the term don't agree on its meaning. Higher quality, sure. But while for some this means a limited bottling from the cream of each year's crop, others save the term for wine so exceptional it can only be made in outstanding vintages. In some cases, it designates small vineyard lots and regional flavor. In others, a wine with aging potential. Some Reserves get special treatment; more time on oak, for example.

Australia and South America are no less slippery on the subject. Europe is a different story. In Spain and Italy, use of the term is strictly controlled. In Spain, for instance, a Rioja Reserva is released only after three years of aging, at least one of them in oak barrels; and a Gran Reserva must age for five years, in wood for at least two of them. Italian Riservas have similar requirements. In France, the term has no legal significance, but you can generally count on a French Reserve to represent the winemaker's best effort.

To keep teeth in the term, the EU will not accept our wine with any quality claims on the label, just the facts. For that reason, some US wineries, intent on making an international splash, are ditching the term altogether. Instead, they highlight something more concrete, like a single vineyard. Another reason they're changing their tack is that quality statements have been diluted to the point of meaninglessness over here.

Glen Ellen's $6 "Proprietor's Reserve," Kendall Jackson's "Vintner's Reserve," and half a dozen different "Coastal Reserves," all make hash of the term. There's nothing wrong with these wines, but they're not exactly special bottlings.

Vintner's Reserve also happens to be the name of a mail order, home-winemaking kit that produces, in twenty-eight days, "wines of great character, with superlative color, flavor & aroma characteristics."

Yeah, right. And in your last job you routinely Infiltrated! Beheaded! Electrocuted! Disinterred!

State of Alert

The nanny label

Warning: *reading wine columns while performing brain surgery may cause lawsuits.*

I'm writing this from Vinexpo, the giant wine convention in Bordeaux, France, where connoisseurs from all over the world come to spit in buckets and jockey for invitations to the coolest parties.

As a proud American, I naturally feel compelled to defend my culture, especially here in the land-of-the-lunch, where the two-hour midday break is considered a religious sacrament. Lately I'm finding my back to the wall when it comes to the health warning we so prudently require on our wine bottles.

"Consumption of alcohol impairs your ability to ...operate machinery. Women should not drink alcoholic beverages during pregnancy." Europeans think this is a riot. We're the kid whose mom won't let him cross the street by himself. We're so stupid we need to be told not to get wasted and play Lego with a wrecking ball. That is, when we're not mistaking our hairdryer for a bath toy.

They're not dismissing the serious consequences of drinking to excess while pregnant or on the road. Fetal alcohol syndrome and car crashes are a tragedy. But more so, they ask, than death by avalanche or on slippery bathroom tiles?

And don't we know the difference between use and abuse? Can't we eat a few chips without emptying the bag? (Frankly, no.)

They make fun of us. "The thing is," confides an Italian journalist when I show her the label, "that's the only way they'd *get* me to drive a tractor."

"I've always thought they should put, 'Don't get women pregnant while drinking,'" says a German winemaker.

A French château owner adds, "Americans don't understand about pregnancy. Pregnant women *should* drink wine. I mean, how else are we going to get our new customers?"

But, surely they'd agree with the additional statement proposed by lawmakers: "Consumption of alcohol may lead to alcoholism." Undoubtedly true, they admit, in a fraction of the population. But danger lurks all around us. Some people are mortally allergic to peanuts; where are the warning labels on Snickers bars? Or on perfume, which causes some people asthma attacks?

If your warning label was any good at all, they continue, it would mention some of the hundreds of studies linking wine and health. They point out a quote from former California governor Gray Davis: "I ran into Ernest Gallo, and he and Robert Mondavi are in their nineties. What does that tell you? Drink wine and live a long and healthy life."

As a matter of fact, I tell them, our winemakers just won the right to add a thing called the "directional label." No, it doesn't actually come right out and say anything positive. But it does hint at the possibility of asking your doctor if there might be anything good about drinking wine. Or, alternatively—and certainly something we've all been moved to do when opening a nice Zinfandel—you could send away for the Federal Dietary Guidelines and spend an afternoon searching for the one, reluctant sentence admitting the possible connection between moderate wine drinking and lowered risk of heart disease.

Naturally, though, these dangerously libertine statements must be balanced by yet more warnings. Any more balance, scoff the Euros, and your bottles are going to tip over sideways.

These people see wine as just part of a meal, with the danger profile of, say, ketchup. "But you guys regulate it with firearms," laughs a wine mogul from Canada. "At least you did until you moved it to, what, the department of Home Depot?"

I try to explain that to Americans, pleasure, in and of itself, is bad. Vacation, flirtation, massage and dessert; all are suspect. We may eat more sweets than they do in France, but we have the decency to disapprove of them. Sanctioned enjoyment, as we see it, requires suffering; the runner's high, for example.

I'm beginning to despair of ever teaching these happy-go-lucky imbibers the true meaning of solid, American Puritanism: the irrational fear that someone, somewhere, is having a good time.

Sleeping Monster

Neo-Prohibition lurks

Anyone who has seen a horror movie knows perfectly well that you never, never turn your back on a corpse, even if it's been shot, bludgeoned and dismembered. Make no mistake; it WILL get up and come after you.

Listen to the soundtrack: that pounding crescendo you hear is Prohibition, and the reports of its death are greatly exaggerated. Au contraire, it's tanned, rested and ready to snatch that glass of Chardonnay from your sinning hand.

The nannies of temperance have been biding their time like sleeper cells, awaiting the right moral climate to rise and rule again. Mothers Against Drunk Driving is fighting for higher taxes on wine and beer, and won't be happy until the blood-alcohol standard is low enough to blow after gargling mouthwash or eating a piece of stale bread.

"American Puritanism: the irrational fear that someone,
somewhere, is having a good time."

Spirits are one thing, but how did wine, a benign part of a civilized meal, become so suspect here that we regulated it along with firearms?

America and wine got off to a rocky start. Though we're home to over fifty grape species (prompting Leif Ericson to dub us Vinland), none of them make serious wine. Over and over, from the earliest colonial times, connoisseurs who knew the difference planted European varieties, only to watch them shrivel and die. They didn't understand that they were dealing with the American root louse *phylloxera*, slayer of Old World grapes, later to cross the ocean and decimate the vineyards of Europe.

Only the moneyed of the East Coast could afford imported wine, contributing to its perception as an elite and special-occasion drink. And as for the rest of the country—well, it's one thing to nestle-in barrels for a damp Atlantic crossing—quite another for them to spend a year bumping along a hot, dusty wagon trail. Wine simply couldn't survive a cross-country trip, which is why John Wayne bellied up to the bar for a whisky, not a *demi-bouteille* of Nuits-St-George.

For a short, golden period towards the end of the nineteenth century, it looked like American wine stood a chance. Railroads linked the coasts. Phylloxera was under control. Vineyards thrived. Then along came the Women's Christian Temperance Union. Carrie Nation brandished her hatchet against the evils of gin and demon rum, but, alas, the Eighteenth Amendment wrapped beer and wine into the package.

Australia, too, was threatened by an active temperance movement and a proposed dry amendment. But shortly before the vote, a fortuitous thing happened. Thousands of soldiers came home from World War One. After years in Europe, where wine was more common than toothpaste, they didn't take kindly to the idea of outlawing what had been one of their few solaces in the trenches. The amendment went down in flames.

The American nanny brigade took note. The Eighteenth was ratified three months before our boys got home.

Prohibition devastated the wine industry. Vines were ripped out and replaced by other crops. A whole generation of potential winemakers was lost. A nascent wine culture, nipped in the bud. When, at last, it was repealed in 1933, beer and booze makers hit the ground running while wineries could only begin to replant.

The "noble experiment" did have a few loopholes. You were allowed to make your own wine at home. Some vineyards stayed in business by shipping winemaking kits around the country. They contained grapes, yeast, instructions and sugar.

The sugar was to drown out the taste of the wine, which was terrible. The wine was terrible because the grapes were lousy. The grapes were lousy because the only varieties that survived being shipped as freight were tough cookies; thick skinned, built for endurance, not flavor. None of your namby-pamby *vinifera* stuff.

A handful of wineries managed to stay in business by making sacramental wine for the Catholic Church. As a matter of fact, a great number of churches sprung up during those years, as did the number of faithful mass-goers. The wine they communed with was sweet.

The fact that it was a good thirty years after repeal before wineries were ready with anything resembling serious wine might explain the popularity of White Zin, coolers and other sugary concoctions in this country.

With the return of decent wine still decades away, and surreptitious, speakeasy-style drinking in recent memory, America developed something of a binge pattern. Rather than a glass or two with dinner at night, the upright American drinks nothing all week, then goes all out on Saturday night. Kids, rather than discovering wine at the dinner table, learn by chugging on the sly with one goal in mind; to get drunk.

Drunken people do destructive things. The sleeping monster doesn't like this. He's stirring in his grave. He is Neo-Prohibition. Be afraid. Be very afraid.

Insidious Menace

Chocolate: the gateway candy

When it comes to the dangers of wine, Europeans just don't get it. Throughout the continent, *bambini, enfants* and *Kinder* are sipping a little wine mixed with water at the dinner table. Just one example of their delusion that wine can be enjoyed responsibly at meals.

But there are others. Take the Valaison Wine and Vine Museum in Sierre, Switzerland. To introduce middle-schoolers to the local wine culture, they've developed a program that assigns every fifth-grader four grapevines to tend. All year, the kids are taught to prune, weed, trellis, and finally harvest. Imagine the consequences! These children are being brainwashed into thinking that farming grapes is honest and interesting labor, when all the time it's leading to the manufacture of a substance that tears at the very fabric of society.

Thank heavens, in America we combat that sort of nonsense on every front. Twenty-two separate federal agencies

"Little chocolate bottles, a classic "gateway" candy, are ruining a whole generation of our children."

spend over \$23 billion a year targeting anyone under twenty-one who might try getting away with a stunt like that.

Not for us, that Euro-trash, devil-may-care attitude toward wine. We're sharp enough to look beyond the flavors, the aromas, the romance, to the real matter at hand. Because as we all know, my friends, that is *alcohol*. And it is bad. A recent study in Texas found that "seventy-two percent of secondary school students had *used* alcohol *at some point in their lives* (italics mine)." You see, unlike their dissipated European counterparts, our American teenagers do not "drink wine." They get serious and "use alcohol." You may wonder if alcohol use in this study could include swabbing out a wound with isopropyl. No matter—our children are just as likely to take a swig from the medicine chest as a sip of wine, anyway, since they well know that both fall under the category of Drugs with a capital D—a means to a bad end.

We still have a long way to go. Consider our lax shipping laws. Do you realize that in some states your ten-year-old could use his allowance to order a case of Screaming Eagle on the Internet?

We must be especially vigilante about *laissé faire* attitudes in the kitchen. European corruption has our chefs, Michelin stars in their eyes, blithely braising, deglazing and reducing with wine and flambéing with brandy. To avoid that sort of irresponsible behavior, recipes published in America routinely explain how to substitute, say, vanilla extract, for the brandy originally called for. Never mind that alcohol boils away in cooking. Never mind that extracts are extracted into…alcohol! What's important is the message it sends.

These issues, however, are just a tempest in a wine glass. Inconsequential, really, considering the much greater danger we're facing. I'm referring, of course, to gourmet chocolates.

Remember those little chocolate liqueur bottles wrapped in colored tinfoil? Thankfully, you won't find them in most States of *this* Union! A classic "gateway" candy, they're ruining a whole generation of our children. Just look at me. Product of an abusive home, where dissipated parents hooked me on liqueur-filled chocolates by putting them in my Christmas stocking, I've grown up to be a wine connoisseur. Shocking, but true.

I have in front of me an order form for Bissinger's French Confections—elegant hand-dipped chocolates, flavored with extracts of Cabernet Sauvignon, Chardonnay and Merlot. The brochure warns in stern language to avoid these treats if you are pregnant, under twenty-one, or operating heavy machinery, but I dare that to deter you, once you've had a taste. Disturbed by the vision of *bobon-vivants* run amok, I crunched the numbers.

It takes three six-ounce glasses of wine, consumed within an hour, to bring the average woman's blood-alcohol level to .05, or legally impaired. Average wine being 12% alcohol by volume, that's 2.16 ounces of alcohol. The extracts used in these chocolates are 3.6% alcohol by volume, there are about fifty chocolates per pound, the filling representing 33% of each unit, or .105 ounces of alcohol per pound, therefore .0038 ounces of pure, raw alcohol per piece! You do the math. Never mind, I'll do it. A mere 568 pieces of candy—eleven pounds per person—eaten within an hour, is enough to make you a danger on the road!

Small wonder these time bombs are prohibited in thirty-three states! Steroids and blood doping are child's play in comparison. For the sake of our children, our citizens of tomorrow, we must lobby to secure our borders against unlawful transport of "hard" candies. Let's see the Europeans scoff at that!

BUSINESS

The Naked Glass

What, exactly, are you paying for?

Is an $80 wine ten times better than an $8 one? Will $2,500 guarantee magic in every sip? How is it that a $30 bottle can disappoint, while your latest $6.99 discovery is scrumptious? Of all the mysteries surrounding wine, price seems to be the greatest enigma and the one people ask me about most.

When you pull off the road to pump ethyl, all that matters is the grade of tiger in your tank. With wine, the bottle itself, along with history, nostalgia, status and many more intangibles come into play. Raise your hand if you've never fallen for a pretty label. All these together represent the *total value* (TV) of the wine.

Strip away all the clues and trimmings and you're left with only liquid. That's the *naked glass value* (NGV). To both values there is a time. The trick is to spot the difference.

A passel of costs lines the route from grape to gullet. How do they affect these values? If you get what you pay for, what, exactly, did you pay for?

"What, exactly, are you paying for?"

Toss a chunk to Uncle Sam, and a heftier one to producer, importer, distributor and merchant. Necessary, but you'll only feel the impact on your pocketbook. PR and ads, however, create image, which is an important part of total value. A big splash at auction, a pour-on movie role, a famous name all add mystique; a thing that's invisible to the naked glass.

Packaging, too, adds TV. Heavy bottles, engraved labels and wooden cases all spell luxury. High-quality cork, on the other hand, can also mean the difference between decay and delight—now we're moving into NGV territory.

Expenses become more relevant at the winery. Careful racking, frequent topping up, tasting, blending and other fussing all separate the artists from the factories, and your naked glass knows it. Costly barrels are to oak chips what fresh-squeezed is to Tang. If your wine spends a few years growing up before it's released, it'll cost the producer both storage space and potential sales. You'll pay, but your glass will thank you.

The world's best vineyards have tightly spaced rows of knee-high fruit, often clinging to slopes that would send a mountain goat into treatment for acrophobia. Tractors and other machinery don't rule there like they do at the vino-matics. At harvest, it takes both fingers and brains to pick out the ripest grapes and bunches. Multiply that for the super labor-intensive, late-harvest wines, whose price shows it. Severe pruning means fewer grapes per acre, but higher yields don't make great wine. NGV costs, all of them.

If that acre is part of, say, a California real-estate explosion, you'll pay for the famous appellation. Meanwhile, your naked glass might be just as happy somewhere in Chile. On the other hand, if the land price reflects a tiny parcel of Shangri-La that produces grapes like no other, that's different. In that case, you pay not just for quality, but for scarcity. If your naked glass has fallen in love with a tiny vineyard in Burgundy, for example, it will pony up with pleasure.

Total Value (TV) vs Glass Value (GV)

Costs	Business Costs			Marketing		
	Shipping	Taxes	Profit for Each Tier	Ads	PR: Auctions, Events, Placement	Famous Name
TV	✗	✗	✗	✔	✔	✔
GV	✗	✗	✗	✗	✗	✗

Costs	Packaging			Winemaking		
	Bottles	Closure (corks etc.)	Wooden Case, Labels	Topping, Racking, TLC	Oak	Storage & Aging
TV	✔	✔	✔	✔	✔	✔
GV	✗	✔	✗	✔	✔	✔

Costs	Grapes		Land		Scarcity	
	Time & Labor	Density & Yield	Fashionable Location	Unique Terroir	Status / Hype	Unique Wine
TV	✔	✔	✔	✔	✔	✔
GV	✔	✔	✗	✔	✗	✔

So You Want to Be an Importer

Why wine costs more here

You're just back from a romantic week in Baklavia, where the wine flows like water at every meal. And it's so cheap! A terrific bottle of Red Grommet runs about $4.50. Someone should import this stuff. Without marking it way up, like those greedy corporations do.

Excellent idea! Why not you? Welcome to your new import business. Let's see what it takes to get a bottle of Red Grommet to market.

First thing is to apply for a Federal import license. It costs $500 a year if you qualify, but be patient, you won't know for three to five months. Next step is to register your office. Even if it consists of a pencil sharpener and a laptop, you have to record it in every state where you're planning to sell. This should take a month or two, and will run you $100 to $350 per state. Some states require you to register each label separately, so you might want to hold off on the Grommet Grand Reserve for now. And curb the wanderlust. If you move your office, the whole process starts again.

Were you picturing Tupperware-style parties where you sold Grommet to your friends? Sorry, but you're not a licensed retailer. You can't even sell the stuff to your favorite restaurant. You'll have to go through a distributor. Your next step, then, is to designate a distributor in each state, and, in some cases, in each county.

Try to give this step a little more thought than you did your first marriage. In the thirteen "franchised" states, you can't drop a distributor unless he releases you. Even if his idea of selling your wine is to let it grow moss in a corner.

Meanwhile, you should be working on your label. The Baklavian alphabet needs to be translated into English. You'll need stern warnings about death and pregnancy and driving a front-end loader. You must declare how much alcohol is in there, admit to the presence of sulfites, and generally make it clear that you're selling a dangerous commodity. Then proofread, pray, repeat, submit to the Tax and Trade Bureau, and wait three months.

Uh oh! Looks like that Baklavian fertility symbol is a little too risqué for Americans. The phrase "Grommet till you vomit," will have to go, too, since laws forbid "any statement, design, device, or representation... which tends to create the impression that a wine has intoxicating qualities." Fix the label, re-submit, and you should get final approval in another four months.

You've dug pretty deep into your savings by now. Can you make it back? Sure! Sell to the distributor at $6.50 and you'll even make a little profit. Still a damned good price for a nice little wine.

But, jeez, it's May already and still no Grommet on the shelves. Better get moving. Your distributors finally place their first order. Your bottles are labeled for you at the winery, and consolidated in a container with other wines. They wait for a ship heading this way, and then it's three to four weeks at sea, and ten more days to get through post-9/11 customs.

July arrives and the big day dawns. You watch proudly as your first case of Red Grommet goes on display. But what's the deal? No one's buying! You start to think: let's see, the distributor sells the bottle for $10.39, and by the time the stores and restaurants have made anything...

As you stand, despondent, in the Balkan aisle, you overhear two guys talking. "Can you believe they want $15.50 for that Baklavian junk?" "Yeah, and $30 in a restaurant! Why doesn't someone import some decent, affordable wine? You know, I was in Frexonia last year...."

Twelve Things You Shouldn't
<u>Know About Wine</u>

What the industry doesn't tell you

The wine industry loves giving out instructional brochures like: "Ten Tips to Tackling Wine." Here's the list they don't want you to read.

Back label tricks:

1) "A crisp, picnic wine, with gobs of Asian moonfruit on the palate and a swoosh of pungent finberry on the long finish..." These descriptions are one part winemaker's ego to two parts PR copywriter's fantasy. Any resemblance to the wine inside, living or dead, is purely coincidental.

2) "Nuances of toasty French oak." Beware references to "oak" without the word "barrel." Barrels cost a bundle. Some wineries save by simply tossing in chips or extract for oak flavor. True barrel-aging, though, concentrates wine through evaporation, adds richness to the texture and helps the wine age gracefully. Done right, it may add no discernible oak flavor at all.

3) In general, the more the winemaker is directly involved in each step, the better. "Estate Bottled" means the same folks grew (or at least contracted) the grapes, and made and bottled the wine on the property. On the other extreme, "Cellared by X," or "Vinted and bottled by X," mean that God-knows-who made the wine and then slapped on X's label.

Front label tricks:

4) What's in a 1997 Sonoma Zinfandel? Laws vary, but all allow ample room for fudging. In this example, only 85% of it has to come from Sonoma, 5% could be a different vintage, and 25% of the grapes might not even be Zinfandel.

5) If you want a status appellation, like Napa Valley, shop carefully. Until a recent court decision, a winery called "Chateau Napa" did not imply the grapes' origin any more than "Caspian Brothers' Caviar" means it's Iranian beluga. There's still mystery Napa on the market, and many other appellations still use this ruse.

Shopping:

6) Important-looking bottles are often heavy. Heft, apparently, adds gravitas, and helps separate you from your money unless you're onto this trick. Another value-adding bottle ploy is to deepen the punt—that dent in the bottom. Then the bottle has to be bigger to hold all 750 mls, so it looks like you're getting more.

7) Bring your reading specs when you shop. "Shelf talkers," the mini-reviews that line the shelves of wine stores, don't always correspond with the wine being sold. You could read a blurb on the 2000 Syrah that got 95 points from Robert Parker, and then unwittingly grab a bottle of the 82-point 2001, the one they're actually selling.

In the Bottle:

9) "Good wine is made in the vineyard," say the winemakers; they are but shepherds, gently herding the grape from vine to bottle. Actually, they add all kinds of stuff. Regional laws depending, additions might include acid, sugar, tannins, coloring agents and, almost always, sulfites. None are problems, most improve the wine, but boy, do they hate admitting it.

8) The recent wine glut spawned a category of super-cheap consolidators, the most famous being Charles Shaw, AKA Two-Buck Chuck. They buy up wine destined for the drainpipe, bottle and sell it for everyday drinking. It's a great deal, but since sources vary, so does the wine. The Chardonnay you buy today might taste nothing like the one you had last month.

Reviews:

10) Sometimes samples sent to reviewers are a special bottling: the cream of the cru. Unless a reviewer buys anonymously at retail, what he tastes and writes up might be quite different from what you buy and drink.

11) Glossy magazines that review hundreds of wines often feature photos of a few of the labels. In some cases, they represent the editors' pick of the issue. In others, they're simply wineries willing to pay for the privilege. It's good to know which is which.

Prices:

12) Here's what's between you and that charming $2 white you had on vacation abroad: a consolidator and shipper, import duty, regulation and licensing fees, an importer, a distributor

or wholesaler, and a retailer or restaurant. That's why it costs $15 to $30 by the time you buy it here.

Congratulations! You know the secrets of smart wine buying. Now I'm going to have to kill you.

Hey Big Spender

Trophy hunter bags big one

This week, *Wine Expectorator* profiles one of the great American collectors: Dr. Ainsworth Teasdale, ear, nose and throat specialist and director of the world famous Nasal Wart Clinic in Fishkill, New York. He was not always a wine aficionado. "I hunted other things, originally. Big game, to start. Bagged my first rhinoceros in my teens, although what it was doing in my teens I'll never know." Asked about his seminal wine experience, the one that made him devote his life to collecting, his eyes grow moist. "It was beautiful. A 96-point wine, second growth, 1959, $230. All my favorite numbers."

His collection is evenly split between Grand Cru Bordeaux and serious Napa Cabernet such as Opus One, Caymus Special Selection and Screaming Eagle. "Cabernet, now there's a man's grape. Big, tough, tannic. Goes well with a USDA prime, well-marbled rib-eye." And other grapes or countries? "You see, that's what I love about wine," he says, warming to his subject,

"It was beautiful. A 96-point wine, second growth, 1959, $230.
All my favorite numbers."

"Variety! You can find good Cabs from Italy, Australia, even Chile. Not that I drink them, personally. But I'm not a snob. You've got your Le Pin and your Lafite, but it's exciting to discover an obscure little label, you know, a fun, every-day Cab for, say, $60 to $70." Teasdale is serious about educating and broadening his palate. At one point he ventured far enough out of his comfort zone to taste a Burgundy (Domaine de la Romanée-Conti, he specifies, the tiniest and costliest domaine in the region). "People go on about Burgundy, but I just don't get it. Bordeaux is clearly better. For one thing, it ages well, which is very important to a collector. It's like I used to say as a kid, Superman can beat Batman and that's the end of the argument." Despite his experienced palate, Teasdale has little interest in blind tasting. "Drinking wine without seeing the label," he explains, "is like making love to a beautiful woman without a tape-measure and a stopwatch. An interesting exercise, but hardly worth the exertion." An avid gourmet, Teasdale chooses his restaurants carefully. "The first thing I look for is an award-winning wine list, the big thick kind. You see, I'm kind of short and I need something to sit on.

"I've got a real advantage," he continues, "knowing so much about wine. With a long wine list, some people get confused or intimidated, and they try to read the whole thing. Me, I just look for the numbers. Spend $600 for a 95-point bottle, my idea of value, hell, you know you're getting the good stuff. The sommelier's impressed. And whether you're out with clients or a date, they're impressed, too."

The bottle he's most proud of in his collection? "You know, I'm pretty good friends with Hamilton McFudders," he says, referring to the reclusive Napa producer of the legendary Fudd's Vineyard Red, the only wine ever to receive a 101-point rating. McFudders is known for his long allocation list and small production. How small? "One bottle," Teasdale tells us, "released each year at $295,000. I'm on the list to get it in 2012."

He's also excited about two bottles of the highly sought after Final Season 2000. When *Wine Emasculator* demoted it from 94 to 92 points, the winemaker killed himself, making the wine instantly collectable. A mark of his prominence in the wine world, Teasdale was recently made a Chevalier of the Respectful Assembly of Poseurs. "C.R.A.P. is a great group. We wear long robes and silly hats and get together over expensive food and open bottles of expensive Cabernet and talk about how much it all cost us and then we reject new members. *Homo magnus—vinum grandum*—Important men drinking big wine—that's our motto."

Part II: Wines

WHITE

Me Tarzan, Me Red

Red for boys, white for girls?

It's not easy being a guy. Just when you've nailed down the rules, along come women, saying, "I'm only drinking red these days," and the message is clear: they're storming the boys club; they're serious about wine.

This can't last! Isn't there something chromosomal that drives man to red wine even as woman is driven unto chocolate? Yes, gender/taste differences exist, notably during women's ping-pong hormonal cycles, but nothing runs clearly along the Red/White fault line.

Actually men flock to red because it's *not* natural. If you're of the male persuasion, and hard-wired to compete, wine is a limitless minefield of opportunities to make a jackass of yourself. Blue-chip reds are a bomb shelter. Anything pink might as well be a big white target on your rear, complete with "Kick Me" sign.

Easy for the wine trade to say, "Forget the ratings, just trust your own taste." They get thousands of chances to develop their own taste.

The thing is—and I've thought long and hard about this—*wine is not about your own taste*. On the contrary, it's sophisticated. (Mandatory grammatical digression: the root *soph*, meaning "expert or wise," morphs right into *sophist*, one who's "deceptive, adroit...specious," and on into *sophisticated*, "deprived of genuineness or...naïveté." In other words, a long way from nature and too clever by half.)

Even the most "natural" winemaking is a far cry from just leaving the grapes out there to ferment. To appreciate conceptual art or twelve-tone music, you've got to override your instincts and sneak a peek at what the other guy is doing. Broccoli, Bourbon and Barolo are no different. We're born salivating at the sweet and gagging on the bitter. It's the fact that you buck nature and acquire these tastes while others don't that makes them valuable.

Most wine drinkers start sweet. White Zin and coolers give way to the gloppier California Chardonnays and then to drier whites. When, at last, you achieve red, there's no turning back. Why are reds more serious? Because so many whites have a pinch of residual sugar. The stuff we're programmed to like. Reds tend not to, and what's more, they've got tannin.

The tougher that tannin, the more you've arrived. Like hacking through your first cigarette, getting into big, gnarly reds takes grit. Reds are seen as more alcoholic (they're not), more complex (hardly), and heavier (nope, but whites are usually served chilled, so they seem more refreshing). Whites are routinely described as light, delicate, subtle. Reds as big, brawny, bold, robust. Throw on a ribeye. Hear me roar.

So what are women—who sort out status by wiser means, such as how fat their thighs are, or the price of their shoes—

what are they doing in Red Square? Blame Australia. They've flooded us with big, extracted, fruity reds; easy to drink and low in tannin. They're neither sophisticated nor macho. Just good.

If red is no longer the prestigious choice, what's an alpha male to do? He has captured the flag, only to find his baby sister folding it. Time for plan B. Dude enough to choke down a huge Cabernet; can he appreciate the complexities of Grand Cru Riesling? Maybe. After all, guys segued from scotch to vodka martinis with no loss of mojo.

Listen up, men. Want to be seriously male? Want to make even worldly wine-writers sigh and swoon? Forget Red and White. Embrace the spectrum. Don't go to a wine tasting and shun the Chardonnay. There's a time and a place for Grüner Veltliner, rosé, Champagne, Sauternes. Ask the winemaker what he's proud of. Ask the chef what goes best with what you're eating. Listen and learn. Now that's sophisticated.

How Grün Was My Veltliner

Down & dirty Austrian wine

The Teutonic obsession with neatness, I'm told, comes from a time when the church could confiscate the property of slobs. As important as a swept walkway, was to be SEEN sweeping it. The legacy lives on in Austria.

"You can tell who is a lazy winemaker and who is not. That's a lazy one," says my host, pointing to a vineyard with grass growing knee-high between the rows. His own vineyards are groomed like a golf course. The first winemaker I've ever met who goes to work in a suit, albeit a Tyrolean-costumy one, this man puts a lot of stake in neatness. His cellars are so pristine in their ancientness that I suspect little men sneak in to crochet the cobwebs and mow the moss. Outside stands an enormous stack of split logs—the work of his sister, an obsessive chopper who steals neighbors' wood when she runs out.

Perfectionism is one reason Austrian wines are so good. Another is antifreeze. In 1985, a few vintners were caught

"The first winemaker I've ever met who goes to work in a suit, albeit a Tyrolean-costumy one."

sweetening their wines with diethylene glycol. The scandal that ensued, eviscerating sales, was a jolt to the Austrian wine industry. They rallied by ratcheting up the quality laws with the result that you can hardly find a bad wine in Austria today.

The most widely planted grape is Grüner Veltliner. (Say "Grooner Felt-leener" or simply Groo-vee, if you're feeling mod.) Austrians love to tell you how GV trounced some famous white Burgundies in blind competition. This vouches for the grape's quality, but it's a little misleading about its character. Burgundy, made from the Chardonnay grape, can be fat and round and over-groomed, while GV is lean and graceful as a whippet.

Grapefruit, pepper, lime and a hint of youthful spritz qualify GV to wash down anything you can think of eating. And then there are the minerals. For years, when I read tasting notes involving minerals (wet slate, granite, chalk) I figured the only rocks were in the taster's head. Imagine the smell of club soda, though, and you begin to get the idea. GV has a knack of sucking up the flavor at its feet, and its winemakers can talk for hours about the relative merits of gneiss, loess and primary rock. But whether loess is indeed more is only relevant when you're comparing twenty-five wines. From our perspective in America, they all just taste Austrian.

Grüner Veltliner ages gracefully, taking on petrol or honeycomb aromas familiar to lovers of Riesling. Some locals only drink it aged; I prefer the racy fruit of youth. The point may be moot; unless you're very patient or plan to fly to Austria, your chances of getting your hands on an older bottle are slim, anyway.

Riesling is also sublime and stony in Austria. It costs more than GV, and far less of it is grown, but it's worth seeking out. Weissburgunder, otherwise known as Pinot Blanc, is also an exciting wine in Austrian hands, but I wouldn't beat my brains out trying to find it here.

Perhaps the most glorious thing is that, unlike German wine with its inscrutable labels (unless you scrute fluent German), Austrian wines are easy to buy. The masochistic will find plenty of regional quality and ripeness designations to memorize, but you'll do fine with just grape and producer. For extra credit, look for the regions Kamptal, Kremstal and Wachau, where the word "Smaragd" will get you a higher-alcohol, richer wine.

In Weinviertel, "DAC" wines have been vetted for quality. They also designate "regional typicity," meaning that rock geeks can opt for the gneisser gneiss of one town over the loesser loess of another, but if you don't care to dig down that deep you'll still get a fabulous, dry Grüner Veltliner. Anyway, there's something odd about a country so consumed with cleanliness spending so much time discussing dirt.

Don't Blame the Grape

Chardonnay during wartime

I nearly had to duct-tape my keyboard to keep from lighting into the proposal to boycott French wine during wartime. But I'm only a wine writer, and not qualified to opine on such complex issues as war and international relations.

No, instead of invasions and foreign policy, let's discuss a soothing, less polemic subject: Chardonnay. The terrycloth bathrobe, the old leather recliner of wines, Chardonnay is getting so damned comfy that, frankly, it's boring. The smart crowd has jilted it and taken to ordering Pinot Grigio.

Even I, ever on the battlefront of my grueling profession, lose morale when faced with tasting yet another Chardonnay. But I'm up to the task. I make the best of it and so can you. As the cognoscenti sweep off in another direction, you can profit from their absence. You see, it's not really Chardonnay we're sick of. It's what they've done to it.

Political pundit George Will observed: "An idea is not responsible for the people who believe in it." It's not Chardonnay's fault that they've tarted it up out of recognition, or even that so many drink it. Why shouldn't they, when it pops up everywhere with the ubiquity of a smiley face? Besides, people can pronounce it, probably due to that "y" at the end, as opposed to most French words, which sort of trail off into the ether when pronounced properly, oblivious of the efforts made on their behalf by brave consonants, shoring up their borders. Sauvignon Blaa….. Cabernet Fraa... Semillo…. What are they waiting for? In America, when it's time to end a word, we go on in and end it!

A lot of what passes for Chardonnay these days doesn't even taste like wine: it tastes like winemaking. Try to remember the kind of September when Chardonnay was not so malo. I refer to malolactic fermentation, the process that replaces the snap of green apple with the thud of a pound of butter. You can further disguise insipid juice with a heaping helping of grilled oak, by way of chips, slats or extract, resulting in the coconut-cream milkshake that inferior producers commonly brandish as a weapon of crass seduction.

In more caring hands, however, the same variety turns out some of the finest wine in the world. Chablis, Pouilly-Fuissé, Corton-Charlemagne…all Chardonnay. If you start with classy grapes, and leave off the flapdoodle, you find a world of flavors ranging from restrained anise, lilac, orange peel and quince in the Old World, to all-out honeysuckle, papaya, mango and fig in the New. While retaining its essence, Chardonnay is a master of assimilating local color, which is one reason why it would be a shame to limit yourself to, say, non-European brands.

You might, for example, look to the wines of France, which are in no way responsible for the decisions its government has made, and should therefore not be punished, anymore than you should punish yourself by forgoing these pleasures or by erecting divisive, largely symbolic, trade barriers.

At this unique crossroads in history, you are about to experience a deluge of Chardonnay, on a scale never before imagined. It is gathering, even as you read, in Australia, in South America, in North America. Prices will crumble before this onslaught.

You might as well take advantage. Let's dispense quickly with the call to lighter whites due to we're all eating gingered pear sprouts these days. You and I both know that in a given week you eat at least two meals that would crush a Riesling like a tank.

It pays to read the back label. Many wines now proudly proclaim their un-oakiness, with names like Metallico and Virgin. "Fermented and aged in 100% French oak" may be a style you're avoiding, but at least it's not a cheapy. Beware, though, the label that evokes oak without ever mentioning the word "barrel." For instance: "Accented by light toasty oak nuances." This is blatant disregard of quality standards. They're not fooling us, and the burden of proof is on them. Not on some namby-pamby inspector who wouldn't know a bag of oak chips if he tripped over it.

I hope this short interlude of wine discourse has helped take your mind off the troubling issues of our times. It certainly was refreshing for me.

Lost in Spice

Gewürztraminer! As much fun
to say as it is to drink

A lot of wine gets sent to my house. I've developed a
certain intimacy with the guys from Fed Ex, UPS and DHL.
They wake me at the crack of 10:30, well before I've readied
myself for sighted members of the human race. When I open
the door, rubbing my eyes and scowling, to their credit, they
never scream.

The federal government requires an adult to sign for wine
shipments. (If there isn't one around they let me do it.) If no
one's home, the wine returns to the climate-controlled
compartment of the truck—guaranteed 100 degrees—where it
bounces over potholes for six hours and then spends the night
in an even hotter garage. After three days of this, it goes back
to the winery where they forward it on to another wine critic.
At least that would explain some of the wines I sample.

I try to tell the guys that they, themselves, constitute an adult. They could sign for me and hide the wine in an undisclosed location known only to them and all the other delivery services. I give them a few bottles and say, "Drink this tonight—think it over." It worked for Don Corleone, but not for me. These guys are incorruptible. I only once got one trained, but he was fired.

If I've failed at bribery, I've succeeded at education. I worked one guy up from White Zinfandel to Barolo and Napa Cabs. Thank God he left the route; I couldn't afford him.

This experience has taught me that the best wine there is for turning neophytes into connoisseurs is Gewürztraminer (gah-VERTS-trah-MEE-ner). Learn to pronounce it and you've got instant cred. It's not that hard. As one Napa vintner points out, everyone can say Schwarzenegger. You know you've got it right when the response is "Gesundheit!"

"Traminer" is the name of the parent grape, from a German/Italian region in the Alps. It's apt to mutate spontaneously, one time resulting in a remarkably fragrant grape that Italians christened Aromatico. The German version: "Gewürz," can mean either "perfumed" or "spicy," which has given rise to all sorts of hoo-ha about Gewürztraminer being a *spicy* wine.

Spicy, to me, suggests meatballs and tamales. Writers go out of their way to find cinnamon and nutmeg in this wine, as well as even odder things like Nivea cream, star anise and Turkish Delight. But what stands up and waves its hand about Gewürztraminer is the aroma of rose petals, litchi nuts, mangoes and other perfume-y fruits and flowers. Smell it twice, and you'll forever be able to pick it out of a line-up with one nostril tied behind you.

Another giveaway is color. The dark pink skins of the grape give it a slightly copper-gold tone. The weirdest thing about Gewürz is that it tells your nose it's sweet, but then throws a change-up: in your mouth, it's bone-dry.

Because the grape ripens early, it needs a long, cool growing season to develop all its complexity and not be just a flabby sugar-bomb. Even so, the grape makes a lot of sugar. Ferment it all, and you get a lot of alcohol, which gives a thick, oily feel in your mouth. That's the classic Alsatian style: aromatic, bone dry, low acid, full body, high alcohol. (Which is why wine writer Paul Gregutt pronounces it "Getworsethanhammered.")

As if it's not complex enough already, Gewürz can get a little bitter on the finish. It's generally assumed in the wine business that Americans do not like bitter. So there's another style: a little thinner bodied, a tiny bit sweet. This is not a bad thing. It's the perfect foil for Indian, Asian, Pacific Rim and, dare I say it... *spicy* food. And it gets seriously jiggy with anything on the barbecue.

Distinctive, exotic, in-your-face, Gewürztraminer isn't an everyday wine, but, get out of your rut, man! I'm always thrilled when the UPS wake-up call includes renditions of this grape, taking me straight from bed to Gewürz.

Behind the Music

Viognier: the rest of the story

This week, *Biography* looks at one of wine's rising stars—a sensuous white grape, as renowned for her troubled background as for her seductive charm, who triumphed over misfortune and won our hearts. A meteoric rise, struggles with leaf rot, a near-miss with extinction. Exotic, enigmatic, temperamental, long shunned by the mainstream, veiled in mystery and tragedy: who is the real Viognier?

Famously coy about her origins, Viognier will only allude vaguely to a childhood in ancient Greece—or was that Rome?—over 2,000 years ago. What's clear is that she arrived in the Rhône Valley around 600 B.C., and that her early years were unscathed by the scars of grafting and clonal selection that traumatized so many of her peers.

A gawky adolescent, her star did not rise immediately. She paid her dues, laboring as a bit player in such productions as Côte Rôtie, a red wine that profits from the intense character of this demure white, though she never appears in the credits.

"Famously coy about her origins, Viognier will only allude
vaguely to a childhood in ancient Greece—or was that Rome?—
over 2,000 years ago."

The hard work paid off. In the pop of a cork, she found herself the toast of France, starring in the critically acclaimed Condrieu, as well as the smaller but equally piquant Château-Grillet. Both appellations still inspire a kind of frenzied passion in devotees.

Beneath the glamorous façade, however, trouble was brewing. She was earning the reputation of a Prima Donna, fastidious and difficult to grow. Everything upset her—the soil, the weather—in fact, only the most patient producers could coax a performance out of her at all. The theatrics were just cover for a much darker weakness. An inherited predilection for powdery mildew held her powerless in its grip. Interventions failed. Sometimes she could hardly produce, and growers watched a season of labor go to waste.

Cherry trees were a safer bet. Besides, there were plenty of grapes willing to work, like the increasingly popular, easygoing Chardonnay. As consumers lost interest, and growers abandoned her, Viognier, unable to master her moods, watched her fame slip away. She grew despondent. By the 1960s she had shrunk to thirty hectares, derided, then forgotten. Would Viognier survive?

We may never know exactly what happened, but somehow Viognier pulled herself together. She was spotted in remote parts of Italy and Spain. Rumors spread of a comeback. Then, in 1981, a couple of California grape-wranglers, scouting foreign talent, decided to take a gamble on her. The battles with mood and mold still plagued her, but New World producers weren't daunted. On the contrary, her high-maintenance personality intrigued them. She doesn't like this soil, this climate, they said; no biggie, we'll move her.

Gradually, she thrived. Loyal fans of Chardonnay and Sauvignon Blanc heard the buzz and came to check her out.

They were astonished by her intoxicating perfume of apricot, pear, honeysuckle, and violet, promising a mouthful of honey, but paying off dry, arch and complex. They marveled at her creamy, unctuous texture, ketchup-slow and smooth as the song of an auctioneer.

No designer oak for her, in fact her only beauty secret was generous alcohol, responsible both for the illusion of sweetness and her va-va-voom body, well developed even when she's fresh and young.

The very best is still devilishly expensive. There have been a few low-budget jobs she'd just as soon forget. But a growing selection of mid-priced Viognier offers a mouthful of luxury for only a handful of bills.

RED

Meet the Pinots

Scandalous grape family

Pinot. The word keeps popping up like Paris Hilton in your spam box. Pinot Noir, Pinot Blanc, Pinot Grigio. What's up with that?

Welcome to this brilliant, dysfunctional family of grapes, whose ancestral vault was recently pillaged by DNA-crazed scientists, to reveal some shocking skeletons.

Named for the pinecone that its clusters resemble, Pinot is one of the oldest cultivated wine grapes. First-century Romans were crazy for it and carried around little papyrus vintage charts; only they kept drinking too early because the years went backward.

Not long after, a Pinot forefather went slumming, crossing paths with a deadbeat floozy named Gouais Blanc. This grape was so awful that the French wouldn't grow it and it was outlawed thrice in the Middle Ages. That didn't keep it from reproducing heedlessly, generating oceans of dreadful wine.

"A grape so awful the French outlawed it thrice in the Middle Ages."

From this sordid union of outcast and aristocrat sprung sixteen of the world's greatest grapes; four of them Pinots: Gris, Blanc, Meunier and Noir.

Pinot Blanc, kind of a low-fat Chardonnay, is charming and affordable. Lithe, crisp, and flowery when young, she develops complex honey tones with age. She shines in cool regions like Alsace and Italy's Alto Adige, and the New World has not been blind to her charms.

But she's a scammer. Like Andy Warhol signing art made by his staff, she gets credit for work she hasn't done. In Alsace, a wine labeled Pinot Blanc can contain other family grapes and even outsiders. In fact, it doesn't require her presence at all.

Pinot Gris is a grape with identity issues. One day she's flabby and bland, the next thin and astringent, or all oaked up like a Chardonnay impersonator. Add to the confusion her split personality: one clone, *Tokay à petits grains*, makes noble, complex wines, but you're much more likely to run into the dull, but prolific *gros grain*, key player in far too much Italian Pinot Grigio.

Aromatically challenged, she makes it up in texture. The best Pinot Gris is dense and sleek like a sea lion, and rarely clashes with food. She, too, excels in Alsace, where they sometimes call her Tokay. Germany and Oregon also transcend her neuroses and coax her to perform.

Pinot Meunier is not the brightest crayon in the box. Low tannin and color makes him useless for aging. But he's found his niche in the family business as a supporting player in Champagne, where he adds acid and bright, fruity notes to the mix.

Then there's Pinot Noir, the heartbreaker. Dashing, full flavored, with mesmerizing earthiness, his perfume and silky texture seduce with poetry where other wines flash credit cards and gold chains. A high-maintenance romancer, he's prone to every grape affliction known. He's temperamental, unstable, a grape of a thousand clones (versus Cabernet's twelve.) Which explains his little perversion: cross-dressing. One day he's a vineyard of red grapes; next he's wearing his sisters' undies—becoming Gris or even Blanc. Hungry for attention, he'll wear red and white berries on the same vine, even in the same bunch of grapes.

Despite this, he keeps company with that gorgeous, well-bred star, Chardonnay. They share vineyards in Burgundy and sometimes the same bottle in Champagne. Yet a shadow hangs over this union. To her intense embarrassment, though she's denied it for centuries, Chardonnay turns out to be a not-so-distant cousin, descended from the same, shameful mating that produced the Pinots. Any offspring these two produced would be plagued with the inbred feebleness endemic in royal families. The robust Gouais Blanc was just the dose needed, it seems, to turn a weary aristocrat into a patriarch of noble wine.

Add Water and Stir

Beaujolais: nouveau & otherwise

Batten down the hatches: the flood of Beaujolais Nouveau is almost arrivé. Fanatics, who queue up with sleeping bag and thermos for Krispy Kreme openings, take note. But, wait. If Beaujolais Nouveau is so great, then how come (you might ask, if you followed such things) thirteen million bottles failed to sell last year and were turned into industrial alcohol? Is Nouveau a victim of its own hoopla?

When you grow something, inevitably you go a little whacko at harvest time. If that something ferments into alcohol, why, then, pagan bonfires and Bacchic fertility rites are in order. After months of backbreaking trellising, pruning, weeding, drinking, crushing, pumping, drinking some more—it's only natural you'd want to celebrate, by, well, drinking.

The party starts in Beaujolais with barely nascent wine, still frothing and fizzing and remembering its days as fruit. Originally, this cradle robbery was a local thing, but word spread and one day the government noticed that Beaujolaisians were having TOO MUCH FUN. Not exactly illegal, all the same fun must be taxed, regulated, slapped around and hogtied like everything else in France except sex. Henceforth, they declared, Beaujolais shall not be fizzy! It will be bottled no earlier than midnight, November 15th! This was subsequently changed to "the third Thursday in November," ensuring a long weekend for celebrants to get drunk and sober up before returning to that crucial job that keeps the national economy running: having lunch.

A brilliant stroke of marketing by *negociant* George Dubœuf in the '70s created the impression of a panic. With a little well-placed PR, he spread the perception that just minutes after bottling, baby Beaujolais was being rushed by Concorde, train, camel and rickshaw to all corners of the globe where people clamored to be the very first to uncork the party.

The sales went crazy, but producers got lazy. "Made early, drunk early, pissed early— paid early," goes the local saying. Shoddy winemaking, over-production and fertilizers that made the wine taste like bananas played hell with a drink that wasn't that special to begin with. The wine got worse, prices fell, winemakers cut more corners, and come last autumn, they could hardly give the stuff away.

At its best, Nouveau is a simple, fruity thirst-quencher. You don't analyze it; you plunge in and do the backstroke. It coaxes rivery verbs out of wine pundits—words like "guzzle," "gulp," "gush" and "glug," (not to mention "quaff," a sure sign it's time to send your wine writer in for a tune-up.) It's often touted as a picnic wine, but, honestly, when was the last time you went on a picnic?

The problem with all this Nouveau hype is that it smears the reputation of REAL Beaujolais. With a little TLC, the Gamay grape (*Beaujolais* is the place, not the grape) makes charming wine; grape-juicy, earthy, with a silken texture. Best of all, it's cheap. Far cheaper than the Burgundy produced next-door.

Look for Beaujolais-Villages, and drink it within the year. Move up a level and you get the stars of Beaujolais; the *Crus*, named after ten specific growing areas, among them: Morgon, Brouilly, Fleurie, and Moulin-à-Vent. Cru Beaujolais ages nicely, but only for three to five years. The perfect cellaring wine for those of us being medicated for attention deficit disorder.

So, party away with Nouveau if you like, remembering that eight weeks ago this was a bunch of grapes on a vine. But don't pass up the super values of grown-up Beaujolais.

Pinophilia

Burgundy, artists & lovers

If you have the capacity to love at all, you've probably loved someone who put you through hell. In fact, there's evidence to show that the wronger they done you, the more you tied yourself in knots to win them. Lab rats learn to calmly depress a lever if they're rewarded with cocaine each time. But rewarded *sporadically*, they press the lever with the zeal of a Vegas slot-player.

Lovers of Pinot Noir, the red grape of Burgundy, will recognize themselves; chasing that first elusive high, seldom scoring. There's nothing quite like it in the wine world for parting fools from their money.

But first: if you're the type whose idea of a good time is analyzing bond indenture account deposit runs to make sure that the negative arbitrage matches the underwritten letter of credit amounts, go back to your Bordeaux and read no farther. Cabernet, they say, is for doctors and lawyers; Pinot Noir for artists and lovers.

"The Burgundian vigneron shepherds his grapes from graft to cork with his own two hands."

Take the growers. Do you suppose the Baroness Rothschild dons overalls and pushes a wheelbarrow around the Mouton lower forty? No way. She delegates. The Burgundian *vigneron*, by contrast, shepherds his grapes from cradle to grave, from graft to cork, with his own two hands.

He has to, because unlike Cabernet, which cheerfully sets up housekeeping anywhere it's put, Pinot Noir is persnickety. Thin-skinned and sensitive, it sulks as often as it thrives. It goes all catawampus if it's not shipped and stored just so. Do doctors and lawyers put up with that sort of crap? No way. They go watch the game.

That leaves the artists and lovers, who know that this is not a grape you club over the head and drag to your cave. You strum a guitar under its window. You lay your coat in a puddle. And when everything goes right—halleluiah!

This attention has begun paying off in the New World, notably Oregon and New Zealand. While they haven't exactly tamed the shrew, they're coaxing out lush, aromatic wine. Beautiful Pinot Noir indeed, but what they haven't got is the dirt.

Lovers of old-world, Burgundian Pinot Noir prefer their fruit with a helping of rotting-leaf funk, sometimes described as "barnyard." And you know what animals do in the barnyard. What could be appealing about this combo of flowers and excrement? Well, your first cigarette, which had you retching and reeling and turning green, didn't show a lot of promise either.

Burgundy lovers speak reverently of their First Time; that defining click: "So THAT'S what all the fuss is about!" Once it happens, your wine life is never the same. You find yourself spending ridiculous sums on bottles that all too often disappoint. Initiates look knowingly at one another while outsiders suspect it's all a bunch of hooey.

I did for the longest time, figuring the people who got all rhapsodic about the stuff were merely wine-snobs. Then one day, in the cellar of Domaine Voillot in Burgundy, it happened. Suddenly, in one mouthful, the mushrooms put their arms around the strawberries and took off in a waltz so dramatic I must have staggered a little, because Jean-Pierre Charlot, the winemaker in question, asked if I was OK.

Once he realized he was witnessing a religious conversion, he began opening bottle after bottle for me. He sent me off with big hugs and a bottle of Volnay "Les Frémiets," which I regret to say I shared with a friend in a hotel room a few days later. I'd bang my head against the wall thinking about it, but, you know, we poets don't collect wine, we make love to it.

The Wild Ones

Syrah & Grenache: don't let them date your daughter

You, who have been ordering "a glass of Merlot" for the last few years, let it be your New Year's resolution to change this behavior. "But I like Merlot," you may say, "it's red, it's smooth, and I can pronounce it. Why change?"

Because, my friend, Merlot is the mashed potatoes of wine. Non-controversial, goes down easy, but—my God!—look at the feast you're missing!

True, Merlot is capable of greatness, notably in St. Emilion, where it's propped up by Cabernets; Franc and Sauvignon. But that bears little resemblance to what you've been drinking, which has been crafted, as if by committee, to offend no one. The vinous equivalent of the emasculated salutation, "Happy Holidays!"

What instead? You may have some post-traumatic issues with Cabernet; the sensation of sucking on fourteen teabags or brushing your teeth with a belt-sander. That's grape tannin at work, and one of the appeals of Merlot is its lack of tannin, which is why people refer to it as "soft."

The hell with Cab and Merlot. Allow me to introduce two grapes that won't exfoliate your tongue, but are a mile from bland. You're probably familiar with the first one, Syrah. Good Syrah is dark, concentrated, and brims with jammy fruit and peppery spice and tar. It puts the Pop in Châteauneuf-du-, and it's the only official red in the Northern Rhône. Australia's been doing it for 100 years, and California's come aboard, too, so you should have no trouble finding Syrah in all price ranges.

Point of order: Australians call it Shiraz. Different style, sometimes, but same grape. Petite Sirah, however, is a different grape altogether. We, in the wine business, encourage this sort of thing because it makes us look smart.

Grenache, my second candidate, is the most widely planted grape you've never heard of. Prolific, easy to grow, it's a staple of jugs and boxes all over the world. Jug-ular Grenache is thin, brownish and insipid. "Labour, not management," sniffs one critic. But there's another side to Grenache. If you torture the grape, deprive it of water, lower the yields, and make it get up off the sofa and work, ah, then… (Caution: irrational, passionate, wine writing ahead!)

Color: close to black. You inhale; a cloud of fruit and spice fills your nose. In your mouth, an explosion of berries. Followed by sweetness, candied, like an apple at a fair. Then, a dark note appears. A flash of licorice. Treacle. Bitterness, like tobacco, washes over the back and sides of your tongue. You feel violated. You love it.

If Pinot Noir is a poet who whispers in your ear by firelight, Grenache wears a black leather jacket and picks you up on a Harley. It's known as a rustic wine, because it's high in alcohol, not too subtle, and mostly doesn't get better with age. I've been called unsophisticated for loving it, but I'll admit it: good Grenache, savage and breathtaking, makes me weak at the knees.

It's harder to find than Syrah, but it's out there. One of the main ingredients in Spain's most important red, Rioja, it's also bottled there as *Garnacha*. In France, it's the backbone of the Rhône appellations Gigondas and Vacqueyras. It also muscles up the local rosés. Italians call it Cannonau, and make quite a lot of it. There's a white Grenache grape, but it's not in the same league.

Do yourself a favor this year, and give Syrah and Grenache a try. If you can find bottlings labeled "old vines," so much the better. You'll be amazed at how good life can be outside the Merlot zone.

Smoke Signals

Zinfandel fits tribal longings

How is it possible, in an era so illuminated and jet-lagged there's scarcely a circadian rhythm left to dance to, that the spell of summer nights still packs such an emotional wallop? As powerful as the late star-rise and the pulsing hum of crickets is the smell of backyard grilling. It sneaks right past the reasoning part of your brain and straight to the brain stem, sometimes known as the heart, emotionally speaking.

It floods you with a longing for the hamburger buns and sliced tomatoes of companionship, digging into atavistic memories of a life that wasn't even lived by you, but by some stone-age ancestor. Of campfire rings and tribes warmer, wittier and less annoying than the people you invite over. And although the eating is never quite as good as the intoxicating aroma promised, the need to barbecue is an unquenchable longing, an intransitive verb that takes no object, that drives you again and again to make potato salad and marinate meat.

"Don't just drink it, paint with it!"

And when that meat makes its entrance, it's time for Zinfandel. Brawny and masculine, it's the perfect foil for the chilled whites and rosés that got the party rolling. Don't just drink it, paint with it. The spicy pungency of the wine folds beautifully into barbecue sauce.

Long considered the only serious wine America could call its own; Zinfandel recently owned up that it's not a native Yank at all, but a genetic twin of Italy's Primitivo. They share a common Croatian ancestor. Cuttings probably traveled by way of Balkan peasant to Austria, and then in other immigrants' pockets to America and Italy. The Teutonic interlude gave us the name Zinfandel, making the grape about as American as apple strudel.

But even if it's not ours genetically, the style is all our own. Think about it: Cabernet is a Bordeaux wanna-be. Riesling takes its cue from Alsace and Germany. Port should taste like Portugal, and sparkling wine like Champagne. But Zin has no Old World precedent, so Americans make whatever they damn well please out of it.

White Zinfandel, for instance. The infamous skinless-Zin is celebrating its thirtieth birthday this year. Why should we be feting this sweet, pink, soda pop that has given both dessert wine and rosé a bad name? Well, it's been the training wheels for a generation of wine drinkers. And it's performed another service as well: the Zinfandel grape has been here since at least the 1820s, and was once the most widely planted grape in America. It resisted both pestilence and Prohibition, being popular with home-winemakers, the only ones allowed to continue production. But twenty years ago, a lot of it would have been ripped up and replanted to a trendier red had the popularity of White Zin not rescued it. Instead, we still have centenarian vines, some of the oldest living ones in the world, from which we can drink the dark red Zins of our fathers.

It's a tough grape to tame. Because bunches ripen unevenly, both harvesting and fermentation are a major headache and can result in hugely alcoholic wine. One successful Napa Zin-maker calls it her "favorite son-of-a-bitch."

"Imagine a family with three kids," she says. "One always does what he's told. That's Cabernet Sauvignon. The next one likes his independence, but is basically obedient. That's Chardonnay. The third is a rebel—you never know what to expect. You tell him to do A and he does B. But sometimes he does A. Unpredictable. That's Zinfandel."

Maybe it's Ritalin, I don't know, but Zin's behavior is improving. Good Zins are dark, jammy and packed with wild berry flavors and spices like cinnamon and black pepper. Perfect for barbecue sauce. And for sitting in a circle around the fire, howling.

A Bubble Is Born

Diplomats explode; Champagne blamed

'Tis better to drink wine than to worship it. But sometimes you have to face Reims, get down on your knees and salaam the Champagne bubble. Or at least pause and consider its wonder.

Both soda's pop and Champagne's fizz profoundly affect their flavors, but the resemblance ends there. Soda bubbles are a foreign body forced in through a tube. But how do Champagne bubbles get there and why can't you see them through the glass?

They form in the bottle, a by-product of fermenting yeast, a process you've no doubt experienced in your own intestinal laboratory. In the mighty Champagne bottle, there's so much pressure that bubbles stay repressed, dissolved in the wine. Enough pressure, says the Guinness Book, to drive a champagne cork 177 feet, nine inches, one day at Woodbury Winery & Cellars in New York State.

"Local dignitaries were disappointed when the Champagne was flat, but they drank it anyway."

Rocketing cork is only one danger of pressure. There's also the risk of exploding politicians. The first tunnel under the Thames was made possible by giant airlocks. The pressure inside had to be enormous to keep the river from flooding in. To celebrate the halfway point, local dignitaries were invited to a dinner down in the construction tube. Everyone was disappointed when the Champagne was flat, but they drank it anyway. When they ascended after dinner, the suppressed bubbles began rising and popping...*inside them*. Some had to be rushed back down for "Champagne recompression."

Normally, CO_2 finds its outlet in tiny air pockets in your glass, where it rushes in and forms a bubble that grows until buoyant enough to float to the top. The emptied pocket refills with more CO_2, and so the process goes.

There are special tools for scratching up the bottom of your glass so it will calve more bubbles, but the latest science says hogwash. To understand why, think about blowing up a balloon. Sometimes you have to stretch it, or find a grownup to start it for you. As it expands, it gets easier. There is a size at which a balloon is simply too small to blow up. By the same token, scratches in glass are too small for birthing bubbles. Wee tubes of paper and vegetable detritus turn out to be the real nurseries; a squeaky-clean glass would produce no foam.

If Champagne dances while beer plods, consider thirty-bubbles-per-second versus beer's ten. Champagne's higher-pressure bubbles expand faster, and rise faster, too. Proteins called *surfactants* also handicap beer in the bubble race. They poke out the side of beer bubbles, creating drag, the equivalent of driving Daytona with surfboards sticking out your windows.

As soon as a Champagne bubble crests, liquid begins draining down and out of its walls. Weakened, it ruptures, leaving a crater on the surface of the wine. Surrounding liquid rushes in from all sides, colliding and sending a geyser up from the center. This is the sizzling, spattering volcano that tickles your nose and splatters your glasses.

Even the sound of champagne is entrancing. Listen carefully, and you'll hear snap, crackle and pop, rather than a steady fizz. That's because bubbles don't pop evenly. They produce an avalanche effect, one pop causing another, until there's a brief lull and it starts over again.

The kick you get from Champagne is not just a delusional fantasy involving Fred Astaire, Paris and all that Ritz. Compared to a control group drinking flattened Champagne, bubble-bibbers' blood-alcohol-level rises higher and faster.

It's true that Champagne, as Shakespeare put it, "provokes the desire but takes away the performance." For men. However, it raises testosterone levels in women, who should then cheerfully set about compensating for the problem.

Which should be more than enough reason to offer your love a bottle or two of Champagne this Valentine's day. Unless you're planning to dine in a tunnel.

Placomusephilia

Psycho-social significance of bubbles

Could you be a placomusephile? Placomusephilia is practiced by over 20,000 French Champagne afflictionados, and yet the condition is all but unknown in this country.

Before I describe its peculiar symptoms, though, I feel compelled to say that it's high time we stopped relegating Champagne to the holiday ghetto. Two-thirds of all sparkling wine in America is downed in December. That's just, plain wrong. The stuff is cold, fizzy and delicious in hot weather. So from now on I will be writing my annual Champagne column in June.

Once upon a time, Champagne and its ilk went with caviar and anniversaries. But that's SO last-millennium. Modern wine lovers pair it every day, with everything. "It's like dipping your toe in the ocean before you swim," says a friend who makes it a rule always to start dinner with something sparkly. More the running cannonball type, I've never felt the need to warm up before plunging into a vat of Bordeaux, but I see his point.

Why don't we drink Champagne more often? Cultural studies point to our ambiguous relationship with the bubble. Consider the pejorative expressions, "bubble-headed" and "bubble-gum music." Both imply a certain vacuous triviality. While a soak in Epson salts has serious, therapeutic benefits, a bubble bath is considered ephemeral and childish at best, if not downright selfish. And that giant pink bubble that Glinda the Good Witch pilots? Imagine someone serious, like Jesus, driving that!

But our derision, sociologists tell us, masks a profound mistrust. Because the bubble, by its very nature, is deceptive. It will burst, and strand us in the end, as the stock-market bubble has demonstrated. What is it but air, wrapped in a fancy package? A rip-off! A con! It subverts good, solid, Mid-West values!

The Champagne-averse would do well to acknowledge and confront these underlying issues. But let us now exit the orange-coned frontage road of digression and reenter the highway of placomusephilia.

If you're a normal person, you've never noticed that it takes exactly six twists to undo the metal cage on *any* bottle of Champagne, *anywhere* in the world. No one knows why this is so. I'm not sure anyone knows THAT this is so, except my friend David, who likes to count, and has carpalled his tunnels opening too much Champagne.

Anyway, that cage is the *muselage*, French for dog muzzle. Take it off and you'll see the *plaque de muselet*, a shiny, metal cap fitted tightly over the top of the cork. Some are enameled in bright colors with the winemaker's logo. Many are more elaborate works of art, featuring animals, portraits or coats of arms. They've been around since 1906, when Champagne-maker Pol Roger realized he had what amounted to a miniature billboard going unused. Like stamps and coins, they've become collectable, and the collectors are Placomusephiles.

I discovered this in a museum in Reims, Champagne, a town noted for its magnificent cathedral and for being the hardest word to pronounce in the French language. (Hawk up some spit, roll the "r," emit the nasal "a" from the baby's cry, "Whaa," and finish with a hiss.)

You could buy ten plaques in a red velvet box. I was tempted for a minute, but then thought that would be like displaying a stuffed elk that someone else had shot. No, I think if you're going to collect, you should go through the danger and suffering of actually drinking the Champagne. To be really brave, do it year-round.

Ice, Ice Baby

Canadian ice wine

To Americans, Canada is a parallel, frozen universe peopled with hockey players, polar bears and cheap prescription drugs. Wine-wise, it's not on the radar. Well, roll over Mondavi, and give Nanook a chance. Canada happens to be the Mecca for ice wine.

Ice wine, in case you haven't met it, ranks among the world's classiest dessert wines, more Châteauneuf-du-Popsicle than Eski-Merlot pie. To learn what sets this sticky apart, let's pay a visit during harvest. Ah, harvest time! Indian summer! Sweat on the brow and dirt between the toes! Singing workers, laden with bushel baskets of bursting berries...oops, wrong harvest.

It's February on the Niagara peninsula; the thermometer's barely cresting zero. In the proto-dawn of 4:00 a.m., shivering figures in fleece and down maneuver mittened fingers through rattling, lifeless vines. Frozen berries are whisked off as fast as they're picked, to be pressed before the sun comes up.

Look closely: these are not your normal migrant workers. I see doctors, lawyers…media types! Someone with a degree from the Tom Sawyer School of Economics has people paying to come up here and freeze their assets off. Such is the prestige of this rare and expensive wine. What's going on?

There are several ways to turbo-charge a dessert wine. All involve dehydrating the grapes. You can dry them on mats in the sun, or let them shrivel on the vine. Very good little winemakers may get a visit from *botrytis cinerea*, the "noble rot" that turns healthy grapes into hairy, scary, shriveled, little sugar bombs. Then there's ice wine.

Repeated freezing and thawing changes the chemical composition of grapes. It concentrates sugars, acids and extracts and separates them from water, which freezes at a higher temperature. If the grapes are frozen solid enough, pressing will eject the water in crystallized shards, leaving behind the intense, aromatic goo from which ethereal wines are made.

This fortuitous discovery was made in Germany, in 1794, when Hans Schnockleputter went on a Schnapps bender and forgot to harvest his grapes until January, by which time they had frozen solid. When worse comes to Gewürz, bad wine is better than no wine, so he went ahead and vinified, stumbling, thus, upon the magic of Eiswein.

The capricious German weather permits Eiswein only a few times a decade. But in the shadow of the Niagara Escarpment (a geologic formation that sounds like it pushed back its chair in a hurry and left), a harmonic convergence of long, temperate growing season, followed by predictable deep-freeze makes ice wine a reliable crop.

Which is not to say it's easy. Leaving grapes on the vine long into January is risky and labor-intensive business. Rain and windstorms, bad mold and birds all vie to make off with the goods. Yields are extremely low; only 5% to 10% of a normal harvest.

Hence, the price. But at least you know what you're getting. To distinguish themselves from unscrupulous Yankees who put grapes in the freezer and pass the results off as ice wine, Canada formed the Vintners Quality Association (VQA), which tightly controls how, when, and at what temperature you can harvest. Scofflaws can't use the VQA appellation and will be put in the penalty box for icing. Right now you're probably thinking, "Hello! Icing results in a stoppage of play with the puck being dropped in the face-off circle near the goalie in the offending team's zone!" But that would be hockey and this is wine.

And extraordinary wine, indeed. What sets it apart from the cloying mass of syrup that defines some belly-button wines is its zingingly high, refreshing acidity. Along with exotic perfumes like papaya, passion fruit and ginger, you get this sweet-tart wake-up-call of fresh lemon and lime. And texture like the heavy, hypnotic, flow in a lava lamp.

Which just goes to show that where there's a will there's a wine, and we ought to look at a map more often.

Andalusian Delusion

Sherry—not your grandma's tipple

You've experienced wine that takes you back—to your honeymoon on the Amalfi Coast, to that musty cave in Mâcon, to the floor of the frat-house bathroom—but can a wine take you somewhere you've never been?

Jerez, for example? "Sherry," to the Brits, it's the Spanish home of the ultimate "you had to be there" wine. To initiates, sherry conjures up bullfights and flamenco dances, lazy siestas and the dark passion of the gypsy soul. It evokes great cathedrals of barrels and practice sessions with the *venencia*, a traditional whalebone tool that requires a deft wrist-flip to deliver wine from barrel to glass.

But if you've never been to Spain, sherry is what widowed aunts in black lace sip amidst Victorian bric-a-brac. Though Jancis Robinson might believe, as a quote in front of me claims, that sherry is "enormously appreciated" by wine professionals, by this one it's "blithely ignored" when not "violently loathed."

For one thing, it's oxidized, a trait this professional proboscis insists on calling a fault. For another, it brazenly defies the adage, "Great wine is made in the vineyard." Sherry's defining moments (decades, really) take place in the winery.

It's there that the juice of the Palomino grape, fermented to dryness and fortified with brandy, sets off down one of two career paths: towards becoming either a light, dry, palate-cleansing *Fino*; or a sweet, dark, nutty *Oloroso*.

The wine that would be Fino is then visited by an indigenous yeast known as *flor*, which covers the surface with a crusty, white cake, protecting the wine from oxygen and giving it a distinct, aromatic tang. Olorosos, meanwhile, get their alcohol kicked up a notch.

After a year or three, both wines find their place at the top of the *solera*—a system of fractional blending in oak barrels that's as much time machine as mellowing process.

Barrels on the floor contain the oldest wine, the stuff that's drawn off and bottled. No more than a third of a barrel is tapped in any given year, and it's immediately re-filled with wine from the layer above, the first *criadera*. That tier, in turn, is topped up with wine from the second *criadera*, one row up, and so on to the tip-top, where fledgling wine joins the ride.

The young wine's odyssey from top to bottom of the solera can last from nine to over 100 years. Due to this confusion of blending, sherry never carries a vintage date. In fact, a recent harvest and summer-of-1830 are likely to show up in the same mouthful.

Dry when it exits the solera, most Oloroso is then sugared up (more so for the American market) with a dose of PX, a hyper-sweet, concentrated wine from the Pedro Ximinez grape.

Sometimes PX is bottled alone as a megawatt dessert wine. Its lugubrious texture makes it fabulous over ice cream, Belgian waffles and selected body parts. Good Oloroso is nutty, rich and mellow; easy for a sticky-wine aficionado to grasp.

Fino, though, I couldn't get the hang of. Bracing and palate cleansing, yes, but with all the gorgeous dry whites out there, why go out of your way to choose Fino as aperitif? "It's a food thing," say the cognoscenti. "Eat Spanish and you'll understand." So I did, after I figured out their advice to "visit a tapas bar" had nothing to do with Hooters.

They're right! My briny Manzanilla had merely been pining for olives, almonds and hard Manchego cheese. The combination sizzles. I hear guitars. I smell blood and sand. You don't have to go to Spain to appreciate sherry, after all! But I hear the siestas rock.

Have Some, M'Dear

Madeira in the mists

You can leave a bottle of Madeira on a hot car seat for weeks without ruining it, and for that you can thank King George III, the German navy and Zarco the One-Eyed.

1419, dawn of the Age of Exploration: Portuguese sea captain João Gonçalves Zarco, sailing around the north coast of Africa, spots what he describes as "vapors rising from the mouth of hell." Screwing up all his courage, he penetrates hell to discover a small, fog-bound island, part of an archipelago lying 475 miles offshore of Casablanca. The fog is important, not only because it will later feature in the opening shot of a *King Kong* remake, but also because it makes the island invisible. That, plus the fact that it's the largest deep-water harbor in the world, and sits squarely in the path of anyone sailing from Europe to the West Indies, makes it a valuable gateway for Portugal.

Zarco names the island "Madeira," which means wood. Then he wipes out every last tree by starting a fire that will burn for seven years.

He inadvertently provides a great service to the wine industry. The volcanic soil, once too acidic for grape growing, is made alkaline by the ashes of burnt forests. Grapes are planted.

Cut to Boston, 1650: Colonists are protesting the Navigation Acts, which decree that nothing enter or leave the Colonies without passing through, and paying taxes to, England.

Just then, Charles II of England makes one of the great political marriages of all time, when his Portuguese fiancée arrives with a dowry consisting of Bombay, Tangier, Morocco, the use of ports in Africa, Asia and America, and lots of money. She also introduces twin civilizing influences: tea and the fork. To show his gratitude, Charles exempts Madeira from England's protectionist policy.

Madeira, therefore, becomes the only wine shipped directly to America, and so acquires totemic status: a swig of Madeira becomes the American patriot's way of spitting in the British eye. Both the signing of the Declaration of Independence and George Washington's inauguration are toasted in Madeira wine.

However, despite the fact that in 1478, the Duke of Clarence, condemned to death in the Tower of London, chooses to accomplish this by drowning in a vat of Madeira—an anecdote I've been trying to stuff into this story for hours—the fact of the matter is that the wine is thin, acidic, and basically tastes terrible.

This changes in 1600, when a cargo ship goes off course and wanders around the tropics for a year because none of the crew can bring himself to ask for directions. To everyone's surprise, this vacation in the sun vastly improves the wine on-board.

For the next 300 years, Madeira is routinely sailed around the world to mellow, sometimes for five years or more. The inconvenience of this approach is brought home during World War I, when German U-boats find these slow wine tankers gratifying target practice. Especially when they manage to salvage the cargo before it sinks. In a quantum leap of technology—no doubt strongly resisted by Portuguese dockworkers unions—the wine industry trades baking aboard for baking ashore.

Today, the wine cooks for three to six months in giant tanks with heat-sensitive locks that alert the government if the temperature gets too high, and then the government comes and confiscates the wine. If that doesn't happen, the wine next ages in barrels for anywhere from three to hundreds of years before bottling. It's so indestructible that someone who just tasted the 1795 vintage reports "it easily has fifty years of life ahead of it." Which is a lot more than the Duke of Clarence had, but when it comes to that, personally, I think I'd rather jump into a vat of Lubriderm and soften to death.

Part III: Around the Globe

OLD WORLD

Brave New World

This glamorous, traveling life

Lufthansa: Denver-Chicago-Newark-Munich-Bordeaux

Amazing what technology can do! Two whole weeks in France, and I won't miss any work, thanks to the Internet! I checked, and everywhere I'm staying has access. It can get a little expensive in Europe, but I've got one week of unlimited DSL at a French school in Bordeaux, either using their computers, or hooking up my laptop. Globetrottin' wine-writer...no strings...how cool can you get?

École Français, Bordeaux

Only three computers at school, and a long line of students. I finally got one for ten minutes and the French keyboard is weird! No QUERTY. Couldn't find A, apostrophe, or period without long search. Sent out some illiterate e-mail. Tomorrow: bring laptop here and hook up. After that...Château D'Yquem?

"Globetrottin' internet wine-writer...no strings...how cool can you get?"

Hotel Continental, Bordeaux

Tried to work on laptop in hotel room. Power cord wouldn't plug; needed foreign adapter. Two bus-rides, three stores, four hours later; finally found one. Can't wait till I get these bugs fixed and can get out to the Médoc!

École Français

School has only DSL. My computer has only dial-up. Spent two hours trying to reconfigure. Couldn't.

Hotel Continental

Tried Internet through phone in hotel room. Planned to download mail and work off-line to cut costs. Phone cord wouldn't plug; needed foreign adapter. Amazing stroke of luck: front desk had one! I'm going to hang on to this puppy.

Hotel Continental

AOL wouldn't connect. Needed to get French dial-up number and couldn't dial up to get it since it didn't have it. Or something. Going to bed.

Café Le Bal, Bordeaux

Feeling much better after two hours at Internet café. Getting used to foreign keyboard. What does it say about the French that you shift for a period, but *not* for an exclamation mark? Ooh la la!! Got to get some material to write about this week. Going wine tasting at last!

La Caunette, Minèrve

Hiding out in Minèrvois mountains. Left laptop in trunk. Lots of wine! Work is a capitalist plot! I'm a free spirit! Damned deadline. Got to get stupid column in tomorrow.

Bastide Rose, Provence

Lost phone adapter I stole from Hotel Continental. Emmanuel at B&B desk found me one. Horrors! My modem port had MELTED. Justice for stealing? Sacrifice to computer gods? Wrote column, copied to disc, took to front desk computer, uploaded, tried to send, wouldn't work. Emmanuel faxed for me. Made deadline! Took whole day.

Bastide Rose, Provence

Begged ten minutes on front desk computer. "Votre ordinateur a effectué une opération irréversible. Il va maintenant s'éteindre," means "This computer has performed an illegal function and will now shut down." Could use some wine. Wrote for an hour today with pencil and paper. Not bad.

Bannieux, Provence

Spent morning in Avignon getting new modem. Computer-end of power cord dangerously frayed. Spent afternoon looking for new part. No dice. It's American, so not available. Tried drowning sorrows in wine at charming, historic village. Saw Internet café. Tempted.

Bastide Rose, Provence

Emmanuel, former engineer, fixed my cord! I think he hates me. Who cares? I'm up and running at last! E-mail, web, whoopee! This roving writer stuff is fun, once you get the hang of it! At least I'll be prepared for next trip. Two days left for wine research!

Pointe du Sablon, La Camargue

Power outage at B&B. Threw computer out window. Tried to hang self with modem cord. Cord broke. Wrote column on rock, using twig dipped in own blood. Put rock in bottle, dropped in Mediterranean. Hope I meet deadline.

The French Paradox

Why aren't they fat?

France, where I've exiled myself for a few weeks of grueling wine research, is a country of mysteries. For instance, why isn't there ever a washcloth, and what do they use instead? Why only college-dorm-room-size refrigerators? Why does Tory Spelling sound profound when Beverly Hills 90210 is dubbed into French? But the biggest mystery by far: how can the French possibly be so thin?

As a wine writer, I'm invited to many lunches, dinners, and some lunches that last so long they became dinners. Day after day, I watch these people shovel in *fois gras, crème fraîche* and *pain au chocolat*. But no one is fat. Not even pudgy.

Americans, when I point this out, respond, "Yes, but their servings are smaller." Baloney. I've stopped ordering the three-course fixed-price menu, staple of restaurant value, because I can barely make it through the enormous appetizer, let alone a main course and dessert. It's also not true, as Americans claim, that the French eat only one big meal a day. Butter and croissants for breakfast, a hearty lunch with wine, and a full dinner with obligatory cheese course is a pretty normal day here. And they don't pick at their food. Collective national memory of wartime privation decrees that everyone cleans his plate.

How do the French explain it? "You Americans eat potato chips between meals and drink Coke all day long. It's a question of eating good, wholesome food, not that packaged stuff." That sounds reasonable, until I realize that their roster of health food includes butter (none of your poisonous margarine), whole milk (skimming strips the vital forces), duck fat and a daily ration of good chocolate. Delicious, maybe, but not exactly a slimming regimen for most of us.

"It's an attitude," they continue vaguely, "you must focus on and care about your food." Give me a break. Tell the millions of Americans on diets that they just need a more enlightened outlook.

What's really bizarre, in a country where a famous chef committed suicide after losing one of his Michelin stars, is that there is no word in French for food. Oh, there's "*nouriture*" and "*alimentation*," which sound more like fodder on a feedlot. There's even "*cuisine*," when you want to get specific. But no…food.

Eventually, the French shrug and say it must be the red wine.

"They walk everywhere," offers an American friend. Well, they walk as much as all residents of car-averse cities do, but they certainly don't exercise. They scoff at this most narcissistic of American pastimes. Go to a gym for *le body-building*? Impossible! Now, a good lymphatic-drainage massage, that's more like it. Sport is acceptable (as long as it's soccer) but just like us, many more of them watch than play.

Maybe it's the cigarettes. From infancy on, they breathe a constant cloud of smoke that makes lighting up redundant.

The Germans right across the Rhine are fat. This is strange because while they eat sausages and *kuchen mit schlagg* (rhymes with clog) they are seriously into exercise. The public parks have swimming pools and calisthenics courses where the French would put chess tables. Germans, however, drink beer and white wine, seldom red.

Perhaps there's a genetic component. The classic Galois is small, dark and lithe, compared to the brawny, blond, German prototype.

I'm neither little nor dark, and yet the damnedest thing is happening! I've lost ten pounds since I got here. My exercise program, draconian at home, has fizzled. I would have starved by now if I hadn't surrendered to fromage at lunch and charcuterie at breakfast (in Germany, straight from bed to wurst). I haven't started smoking, so that leaves the red wine. I obviously don't drink enough back home.

If you, too, would like to trade Atkins and The Zone for the French Paradox diet, I'd suggest a soufflé of cream, eggs, cheese, butter and goose fat washed down with French wine. It worked for me!

The Feminine Mystique

French winemakers love women

I hate it when the game comes on. All the men instantly lock onto the screen instead of paying attention to ME. That's why I love French wine. Or, more accurately, French winemakers. They like women. They're fascinated by women. They cannot talk wine except in feminine terms.

Jean-Noël Fourmeaux, ebullient Bordelais owner of Chateau Potelle in Napa, explains to me why he doesn't chase ratings (although, boy, does he get them): "It's like the Miss America Pageant; always the girl with the big curves, the big hair, the big lips stands out. The small, graceful girl gets lost." I'm picturing Anna Nicole Smith in the role of California Chardonnay.

Jean-Pierre Charlot of Domaine Voillot in Volnay, Burgundy makes unearthly Pinot Noirs. How much French oak do his wines see? "It's like makeup on a beautiful woman," he says, "a little bit frames and enhances her beauty. Heavy

"This sophisticated, complex, beautiful woman is hooked on France."

eyeliner, blue eye shadow…too much!" It blows me away that even straight Frenchmen know the difference between shadow and liner.

Jean-Yves Bizot of Domaine Bizot, Vosne-Romanée, represents the scientific new generation in Burgundy. He doesn't seem like the passionate type. He tends toward the musical metaphor. Oak is the drum that anchors the symphony. Wine is for drinking, not collecting, just as a Stradivarius does no good hanging in a museum. But he begins to warm as he describes Pinot Noir evolving in your mouth. "It's no good tasting only cherries. First cherries, then raspberries, then strawberries must unfold over time. Like a prism, a crystal, reflecting 100 facets." Finally the national tendency erupts, "It's like a mysterious woman, whose mood is always changing. Voilà." Strangely, my ex-husband never saw this as a positive trait.

The mysteries of both wine and woman entrance these guys. To illustrate that the first impression of a wine may fool you, Fourmeaux tells of handsome man he saw on the subway, proudly holding hands with an enormously fat woman. "What does he see in her?" asks Fourmeaux, "Then I realized: he must know something about her I don't." His face goes dreamy as he imagines possible hidden charms.

He segues, then, to large, corporate wineries, and their consistent, homogenized product. He prefers the artisanal approach: allowing grapes to dictate an ever-changing style. Why? "Think of clothes," he says. "A man wears the same thing every day—pants; a shirt—boring! But a woman! She can dress so many ways. Always a surprise."

Not all wine is feminine. Blair Taylor of the Barolo Grill describes his Gagliardo Barolo as, "Burly, masculine; the kind of wine that'll take out the garbage and pull your car out of a ditch." Make no mistake, though. This wine is ITALIAN.

The absolute cherry on the gateau, as far as I'm concerned, is the French attitude to the *femme d'un certain age*. Fourmeaux, again, on why a fifteen-year-old Bordeaux should not taste like a young, firm, fruity Cabernet: "It's like a woman," he begins— but, of course!—"She should not try to look like a fifteen-year-old when she is fifty. A fifty-year-old woman is sophisticated, complex. She's grown into her beauty."

That does it. So what if they eat lunch all day instead of working? I don't care. Go ahead, praise other countries' wines. This sophisticated, complex, beautiful woman is hooked on France.

Faster Than a Speeding Claret

Super-Tuscan to the rescue!

It's a bird! It's a plane! It's Super-Tuscan! You've probably heard the name; maybe even had a bottle. But what is it, exactly, and what, besides the price tag, is so Super?

Italian wine law is strict but simple, and can be summed up like this: Don't Change Anything, Ever. If the government had its way, Italians would still be stomping grapes with their bare feet, instead of charging tourists to do it for them as part of a "purifying spa experience."

The Super-T phenomenon has its roots in World War II, which remains a haunting, traumatic presence in the European psyche, kind of like senior prom to Americans. In 1939, as Marchese Mario Incisa della Rocchetta of Tuscany, cousin of the famed Antinori family, winemakers since 1385, tried to read this sentence, he got tangled up in modifying clauses. Let's start again. As he watched the Germans march resolutely (is there any other way to march?) into France, a profound fear

"It's a bird! It's a plane! It's Super-Tuscan!"

gripped his entrails: he wouldn't be able to get any more Bordeaux. Strange sentiment, perhaps, for an Italian, but frankly, he preferred Bordeaux to the thin, acidic Chianti of that era, which you remember from your college days, when you used the straw-covered bottle as a candleholder.

Traitor to his culture, the Marchese planted some Cabernet cuttings, copped from Château Lafite Rothschild. The resulting grapes were vinified along with the native Sangiovese and aged in small oak barrels. By the 1960s, the Marchese was producing excellent wine indeed, and he decided to sell what he and his family couldn't drink. However, the powers that bestow the coveted *Denominazione d'Origine Controllata* quality designation weren't having it. "Your wine is made with French grapes, in French barrels!" they told him. "Not only is it not Tuscan, it's not even Italian!" No DOC for him. In fact, he'd have to call it "Table Wine," which was a little like branding "Alpo" on a Morton's steak.

In an attempt to stand out in an ocean of mediocre table wine, as well as justify higher prices, the Marchese christened the wine *Sassicaia*, after its vineyard, and released it in 1968. Soon, his nephew, Piero Antinori, got in the act, with his similarly styled *Tignanello*. *Solaia, Ornellaia,* and a raft of other *'aia*s appeared as more Tuscan winemakers followed suit.

It was the American press who corralled all these names under the heading Super-Tuscan. It refers specifically to a non-DOC blend of Italian and French grapes, made in the International Style, i.e., clean, ripe, fruity, oaked—high quality wine, respectable anywhere, but, as the DOC pointed out, hardly Italian.

In 1995, *Sassicaia* finally got respect, becoming the first single-vineyard DOC in Italy. The rest of the Super-Ts are designated *Indicazione Geografica Tipica* (IGT). The phrase

"Super Tuscan" rarely appears on the label, so look for "IGT," the word *Tuscany* and grape names you've heard of. And, of course, the Kryptonite bottle.

From the Tuscan Trenches

Sweating through Chianti Classico

I have become my own swamp cooler. Sweat sheets down my chest and evaporates in the Tuscan breeze, while I top up my tank with endless bottles of Pellegrino. It's an efficient cycle.

I'm a journalist embedded in Italy, specifically in a bus that could use a set of shocks. We wind up and down and around vertiginous hills, past Roman villages and Cyprus trees, and I find myself more carsick than I can ever remember. Thankfully, the antidote, a stiff shot of Grappa, is always close at hand.

I have to endure this sort of thing in my business—along with three-hour meals on the terrace of a villa overlooking olive groves, vineyards and infinity-edged pools, not to mention the smoldering glances of bare-chested vineyard workers that start me daydreaming of an afternoon under the Tuscan son—all this, to bring you the news from Chianti Classico.

Classico is not a statement of style or quality. It's an area within the region of Chianti, which is inside the larger region of Tuscany, located high on the shin of the Italian boot.

The news you need to know involves one grape, two wines, and an argument. The grape is Sangiovese, a medium-bodied red that acts homesick outside of Italy, but thrives here. The first wine is traditional Chianti Classico, mostly Sangiovese. The second, known as Super Tuscan or IGT (a kind of rebel appellation) adds French grapes, like Cabernet Sauvignon and Merlot, to make a Bordeaux-style blend.

The argument is about progress. Everyone agrees on moving beyond your father's Chianti, the thin, acidic stuff in a basket that Hannibal Lecter paired with fava beans and human liver. They're all happy to ditch an old law requiring the addition of white grapes, left from the days when the red ones were too alcoholic and rough to go it alone.

But then, on one side, you've got the traditionalists, who worry about losing the distinctive local tang and ending up with a homogeneous, "International" wine. On the other side, the modernists, who claim traditional wines were often pretty lousy and that modern techniques can only improve them.

Back on the bus, my stomach and I have noticed that while our driver insists on getting from point A to point B by way of the other 19 letters (mercifully, Italian has no J, K, W, X, or Y), he lets loose an impressive stream of curses each time another car dares to share the road and impede his herky-jerky progress.

Apparently this contrariness is part of the Tuscan character. Ask five Tuscans, the saying goes, and you get six opinions. I hate to spoil a good argument, but I can't help noticing a similarity in the two wine camps. I've seen Classicos rounded out with Merlot and new French oak. I've tasted Super Tuscans that see no wood at all and are 100% Sangiovese.

And no one's in danger of losing the local character. The imprint of *terroir* in both wines is unmistakable. There's the earthy aroma that bursts up at you with the force of a tub of salad dressing opened at 21,000 feet. There's the mouthful of concentrated berries and dark things, like chocolate and tobacco. But a beat later, when you swallow, the wine clamps down on your tongue like a vice, squeezing out the fruit and leaving you with a mouthful of dusty tannin and acid.

However, as anyone can and inevitably will tell you—next one who does gets a smack in the terrazzo—Italian wine is made for food. It's an amazing chemistry experiment. The fat, sugar and salt in a bite of food spackles right over the crack in the wine, leaving you with the impression of a smooth, fruit-filled finish.

The great wines aren't cheap. But worldwide competition this year in the price/value department has some producers goosing up their entry-level line with grapes and wine meant for prestige bottlings. So, whether your kitchen is *molto sofisticato* or more in keeping with *La Dolce Velveeta*, there's a bottle of Tuscan wine for you.

Einz, Zwei, Dry

Decifering German Riesling

Hooray, hoorah, it's asparagus season in Germany! How (and more to the point, why) they manage to transform what should be a thin, green, crunchy vegetable into thick, white fingers of mush is just one of the bafflements of my trip last week to this otherwise charming and hospitable country. Mysterious, also, that shoe stores display only beige, orthopedic clunkers, as though the entire population was in training to become geriatric home-healthcare workers.

And then comes the enigma of German wine; at once easy to drink and impossible to understand. I tasted a breathtaking range of extraordinary wines, from dry to sparkling to mega-watt sweet. There's Goldtröpfchen in them thar hills. You should be buying it. But I'll be damned if I can tell you how.

You're probably skittish about the whole business, after gambling good money on an inscrutable gothic label and ending up with semi-sweet, insipid treacle. Germany is still sending us those wines, because it thinks we want them. We don't. We're a nation of sophisticated Chardonnay drinkers in search of something racy and new.

And, oh! does Germany have it! People often ask me to name my favorite wine, which is a little like asking a parent which is his favorite child. The answer, naturally, is that you love them all, but at any given moment you're rather partial to the one who just put his plate in the dishwasher, and would like to strangle the one who phoned you last night asking for bail.

At this particular moment for me, German Riesling just cleaned its room and took out the trash. It's a one-two punch of screeching lemon-lime acidity, followed by perfumed flowers, peaches, apricots and cream. Like being slapped up the side of the face with a wet trout that morphs into a mermaid. From the hurts-so-good whip-crack of youth to the diesel-oiliness of maturity, these wines keep you guessing, salivating and raving. And with a third less alcohol than most table wines, they also keep you walking straight.

Which version is in which bottle? Your chances of learning this from the label are slim to Blue Nun.

You loved the Federal Budget! You thrilled to the US Tax Code! Now experience the German wine label!

Start with the legal stuff, long Teutonic words denoting village, vineyard and region, as well as words like Kabinett, Spätlese and Auslese, representing ripeness categories, any of which can be dry or sweet.

Layered over this, you've got a gaggle of voluntary classifications, all intended to "simplify" the experience. In one system, dry wines are labeled "Classic," and better dry wines, "Selection." In another they're called "Charta." Then there's the VDP, an organization of high-quality producers whose new system is a jungle the average consumer couldn't hack his way through without filing an environmental impact statement. Nineteen wine journalists from around the world, we sat through two hours of multi-media presentations and still didn't get it.

Actual dialogue:

Q: Will there be anything on the label saying whether the wine is sweet or dry?

A: No, it's not written on the label. We *communicate* it.

Q: Are the classification requirements you're describing different in different regions?

A: No. They're the same all over. With regional variations.

Once upon a time, a marketing whiz doubled his company's shampoo sales by adding one word to the label: "Repeat." I believe Germany could quazillion its wine sales if they'd just suck it up and add three little letters, "DRY."

I intended to return from Germany with a neat rule of thumb to help readers march fearlessly into the German wine section and emerge with a lovely, dry Riesling. I have failed.

This is a shame, because you have got to try these wines. For one thing, they're great with asparagus.

Clues for Finding Dry German Riesling

1) A capsule marked "VDP" = quality. If the label says either "Grosses Gewächs," "Erstes Gewächs" or "Erste Lage," it's dry.

2) "Charta."

3) "Classic" or "Selection"

4) "Trocken"

5) Pfalz region; most are dry.

6) Ask your wine merchant or sommelier.

Latitude Adjustment

Late harvest in Germany

Force-fed Wagnerian opera as a child, my sister Robin turned into Brünhilde. She spent kindergarten in a breastplate, brandishing a spear and singing "Hi-Oh-To-Ho—Oh!" By first grade, she had dropped the Valkyrie and become Jesus because, she explained, "People felt sorry for him." My somewhat less dramatic response to *die nibelungen* was to identify German as the language of love. Listening to parents give their children what-for here on the streets of Rüdesheim in the Rheingau, though, it sounds more like the language of strep throat.

If so, no problem. We're in the land of the most gorge-caressing dessert wines on earth.

For some reason, Americans are very suspicious of sweet wine. OK, I know the reason and it starts with a White Z... It's as if you clawed your way up the ladder of success and finally joined the country club and along comes Uncle Cletus, asking

"Grab your iPod, go lounge by the surf, and by the second day, you're relaxed, bronzed, and stupid."

for a handout in front of all your friends. All sweet wines are not Uncle Cletus!

If you claim you don't like dessert wine, think, for a moment: what do you smell and taste in the wine you love? Black cherry or cola, maybe? Currents? Licorice? Chocolate? If you've got taster's block, perhaps grapes? Sweet things, all. It's not sugar that bugs you, it's balance.

To work on a level beyond Mrs. Butterworth's, dessert wines must maintain a dynamic tension of alcohol, fruit, sugar and acid. Consider the last two: lemons alone are cruel and sugar is cloying, but lemonade transcends the sum of its parts.

Germany is uniquely situated to produce that tension. In the center of Mainz, ground zero of the German wine route, stands a statue of homeboy Johannes Gutenberg, the first person to look at a wine press, slap his forehead, and go, "Hey, that might work with ink!" Next to him runs a metal strip in the pavement, representing the fiftieth parallel, which also happens to bisect Newfoundland. We are seriously North.

There are many ways for sun to ripen a grape. Say you're on vacation in Hawaii and you want to get a tan. You grab your iPod, some SPF and a paperback, and go lounge by the surf. By the second day, you're relaxed, bronzed, and stupid.

Now suppose you get that tan in Newfoundland. You strip down gingerly under the feeble sun, clutching some more substantial reading. Three months later, the Speedo lines are finally coming up. You've finished *The Decline and Fall of the Roman Empire* and are well into Britannica, volume E–F. You're tan, well-informed and extremely irritated. Or, as we say in the wine business, complex and acidic.

Auslese, Beerenauslese, Trockenbeerenauslese and Eiswein are lovely terms to roll off the tongue (if not very lucrative when you're getting paid by the word). They are all sweet, or "late harvest" wines, so called because the grapes are picked in multiple passes through the vineyard, and only the ripest, most concentrated berries are selected. Eiswein is made when repeated thawing and freezing of grapes separates the tasty parts from the watery ones.

The amount of labor involved, the threats (often realized) of hungry birds, diluting rains and disease, as well as the tiny yields, all add up to a product as rare and elusive as hummingbird tears. But then it's not made for chugging. For enlightenment, you need only a small hit, as my cable guy puts it.

Dr. Wilhelm Franke of Weingut Schumacher in Pfalz calls his Eiswein "the textbook" for his estate. "All the flavors you'll find here are concentrated in it," he tells me. In other words, one sip and you've tasted his whole catalog in microcosm. "I hope I didn't put your buds of taste too much under stress," he says as I wonder at this concept. My buds, as a matter of fact, are rolling down a coaster of honey, peach and candied orange peel and swooping back up in a lemon-lime burst. The wine moseys around my mouth with the ambiguous solidity of a jellyfish. I cannot recall a similar sensation that is legal.

It's a mystery and a joy that these wines can be at once so sweet and bracing. Even more of a mystery is how the same people who profess to distain dessert wine make it disappear so fast at my dinner table.

NEW WORLD

Andean Summer

Report from Chile

Australia has its kangaroos, its koalas, and Crocodile Dundee. Spain has fiestas and siestas. Argentina has the tango and Eva Peron. Chile has…wait, give me a minute.

Here's what most Americans know about Chile: it's down there somewhere (would you believe two time zones EAST of Miami?), it's skinny, and it's supposed to be spewing out fabulous wine deals, only you never seem to find one.

With no sexy image, not even a cuddly animal to represent it— tarantulas need not apply—Chile relies on its wine alone to lure you past aisle upon aisle of other countries' offerings. But when was the last time you said, "I really feel like drinking Chilean tonight!?" And what would that mean?

Having no clear idea myself, I flew down to Santiago to investigate.

Chileans are warm and welcoming people, and they show it by offering you *cherimoya*, what a pineapple and banana would produce if you allowed them to mate, at every meal. It's kind of amazing that there ARE any Chileans, considering the number of them that walk up the middle of the highway at rush hour, selling ice cream or juggling, seemingly oblivious to traffic bearing down all around them. Perhaps it's this determined spirit that keeps them improving their own grape strains, an exacting process called *massal selection*, instead of caving in to the "International Style."

International quality is another thing. After centuries of making and drinking their own so-so wine, Chile looked outward and got serious, which meant hiring consultants, ripping out vines, replanting different varieties at higher densities and lower yields, pouring money into operations, and generally doing what it takes to play in the majors.

Their wine country is a series of achingly beautiful valleys tucked between the Andes and the Pacific; heated by one, cooled by the other. Some vineyards line valley floors, while others cling to treacherous slopes. Two opposing theories of viticulture, but, as with circumcision, people tend to root for what they've got. The climate is the kind grapes fantasize about retiring to. Being relatively bug-free, they have vines that predate *phylloxera*, the root-louse that decimated most of the world's vineyards a century and a half ago. Organic farming comes naturally in a place where pesticides aren't a given.

If you stop to notice the sorts of things growing around the vines—eucalyptus, herbs, peppers—you'll pick out their flavor in the reds. The fruit may strike you as restrained if not totally AWOL, especially if you're used to New World juiciness, and what fruit there is can sometimes be eviscerated by tannins. But when all goes right, the reds are elegant and supple, with a decidedly Old World accent.

They're betting on their signature grape, Carmenère, to hook the public's imagination. An obscure blending grape brought over from Bordeaux and then forgotten, Carmenère lay hidden in plain sight for 150 years, pretending to be Merlot, until a visiting botanist did a double take one day and the rest is history. They like this story in Chile, and vineyard managers will not miss an opportunity to show you how to tell the two vines apart. I'm not sure that what the drinking public needs is yet another grape, but we'll see.

The whites, particularly from the Casablanca Valley, are both more exuberant and more reliable. If New Zealand Sauvignon Blanc feels like a James Cagney grapefruit-facial, in Chile he'd use a tangerine. All the zing, plus tropical warmth. And if you've sworn off Chardonnay because of the buttery blandness of it all, the Casablanca variety might entice you back. It's pure, zingy, multifaceted fruit, often un-kissed by the oak fairy.

After you've tried a few, it won't take a gimmick to head you down the South American aisle anymore. All the same, I think Easter Island could supply the face of Chilean wine: enduring, impressive, inscrutable. Rooted in the past; its gaze fixed firmly on the future. Bet you didn't even know it belonged to Chile.

Don't Cry for Me

Romance & clutzery in Argentina

"The Mayan civilization had a notable architecture," says my elementary Spanish book. Why don't they ever offer something useful? It's always post offices, train stations and history, when what you need to say is, "What code do I dial to get my laptop on-line?"

I've tackled a few languages, but I've managed to avoid Spanish. It just never sang to me. Until I went to Argentina. Visiting the wine country around Mendoza was one romantic scene after another, until the cumulative aura of glamour and warmth persuaded this reluctant learner to start conjugating.

There was the love poem, by García Lorca, recited over dinner at Bodega Valentín Bianchi to the soft strumming of guitars, that conveyed such drama and passion that I choked up despite not understanding a word.

And the dashing, sloe-eyed export director who told me that even after ten years of marriage, he and his wife share wine out of the same glass every night at dinner.

"The challenge is to separate the romance from the wine."

Let's not forget the tango, although I'd sort of like to, seeing as my one shot at it, I tripped all over my own feet and those of the poor gaucho trying to steer me. The legs of a tangoing couple are featured on a hologram wine label from Bodega Norton. When you rotate the bottle, they dance. Apparently you can locate their wine in a store because there's always a small knot of people swaying from side to side to see the illusion.

The challenge, for a journalist, is to separate the romance from the wine. Even the vineyards will seduce you. Especially when they're grown on *parral*, an overhead canopy that begs a couple to stroll down its shaded corridors, holding hands, and whispering secrets. The system gets grapes up off the ground so they don't freeze, and provides both sunlight and protection, but because it's labor-intensive, you seldom see it in the US. Workers, however, are plentiful and cheap in Argentina, one reason their wine remains affordable.

José Zuccardi, director of Bodega Familia Zuccardi, cares deeply about his workers. He employs over 400, and insists they go to school at night and get their high-school diploma. He promotes from within, and gives migrants work to do year-round. In his opinion, *terroir*—the distinctive imprint a place has on a wine—is as much about people as about land.

Tradition is important as well. Escoriheula, the only winery left in downtown Mendoza, continues a sweet one: they keep a huge keg of wine, fitted with seven taps, and every Thursday local people can come in and fill up their own jugs and bottles from it.

The Mayan temple that houses Catena Zapata, and the amphitheater at Bodega Salentein, which looks like a good place to go if you want your molecules rearranged and beamed to another planet, are more impressive than romantic; it's their reverence for local stone that gives them warmth.

The only thing that's not particularly romantic is the empanada, but I love it all the same. A half-moon pastry filled with meat or potatoes, it's the sort of thing you could put in your pocket and go down and work in the coalmine all day.

Hard as I try to stay detached, my tasting notes read "generous, accessible, sensual." They describe fruit as "voluptuous" and "full." The whites are lively and complex. Reds can be austere, but are just as often a mouthful of gorgeous, exuberant fruit, much more than you'd expect for the price. Seek out their signature grape, Malbec, as a substitute for good old Merlot and Cabernet. A shipping manager tells me that Malbec, to her, is the sexiest wine of all, because with every sip it gets better. I give up. *Quiero ser romántica.*

Cape Crusaders

South African renaissance

If your teachers frequently pointed out the gulf between your potential (bright) and your grades (dim), then you can relate to South Africa. A few years back it was voted most likely to succeed as the new price/quality Mecca. Yet, Australia, New Zealand and South America sprinted ahead while South Africa was still tying her sneakers.

What happened? They've got fabulous weather and geography. Land and labor costs are low. It's not like winemaking is new to them; they've been at it for centuries. Aha—that's exactly the problem: an entrenched tradition of lousy wine.

It started in the 1500s, when the Dutch spice trade required something of a commute. You think forty-five minutes on the freeway is bad, try a year and a half on the high seas: "We got a roll-over shipwreck blocking traffic in the Mozambique Channel; looks like pirates are already on the scene. Spice traders, you might want to think about the trans-Saharan route, or maybe spend a few more months over your mead before heading out there. But, hey, it's seventy-six and sunny, a great day for discovering new routes to the Indies, right Dave?"

Where do hungry galleon crews go for a few dozen cattle and a cuppa Joe? The Cape of Good Hope, truck stop to the Spice Route. It wasn't long before a Dutch entrepreneur planted grapes and put wine on the menu. Blessed be the Dutch, for they gave us chocolate. But put them in the vineyard and they know not what they do. Grim as their wines were, with no competition for the nearest 700 miles, they sold anyway.

Enter the French, in the form of Huguenots—surplus Protestants kicked out of France by Louis XIV. Born-winemakers, they revamped everything from vine to press, and then proudly sent the resulting wine off to England to be judged. It was awarded Worst-of-Show, along with the tasting note: "Irritates the bowels."

When a group of soldiers died from drinking the stuff, a government taster was appointed for quality control. Now, to be fair, it's the rare wine that can survive a long, bumpy voyage across the equator without refrigeration. Unless it's fortified, along the lines of port or sherry. It was this category that finally put South Africa on the map, notably with *Constantia*, for many decades the absolute hippest dessert wine in Europe.

This ended when Britain, during a rare lull in fighting with France, lowered what had been pretty high tariffs on Gallic wine. The English switched over, and South Africa lost her foreign market. The final blow was the arrival of *phylloxera*, the root louse that decimated the vineyards of Europe. Most South African wineries just folded up and quit.

Emergency life support came in the form of the KWV, a co-op that kept growers churning out masses of jug wine for most of the 20th century. This period is perhaps best remembered for Lieberstein, the White Zin of its day, and top seller in the world for a time.

In 1994, apartheid and associated boycotts ended. The KWV loosened its control and a new appellation system was created. Could South Africa finally make a world-class wine? They underestimated the world. By now, the competition was so fierce and so good that Cape wine hardly registered.

So they retrenched, replanted, rebuilt and spent a lot of money. Although there's still some sorting-out to do of what to plant and where, results of this second wave look very promising.

Pinotage, a hybrid of Pinot Noir and Cinsault, was once the signature grape of South Africa. Now it's losing ground to Cabernet, Syrah and the usual suspects. Chenin Blanc might see the same fate, jilted for the more famous Chardonnay and Sauvignon Blanc.

Values abound, but you know how this cycle works: a country of musty, trusty, traditional wine wakes up and smells the money. Where peasants once guzzled indifferent red and tap-danced in the crushing bin, now pneumatic membrane presses pump next to stainless steel tanks and French oak barrels. Valleys of bushy vines give way to tortured rows of few and fine grapes. In come the critics; up go the prices and quality. The trick is getting in somewhere between Best Buy and Cellar Selection.

When Worlds Collide

Australia through Italian eyes

"That's no Barbera!" scoffs a journalist I'm traveling with in Australia. Enrico Viviano, director of Radio Toscana in Florence, has been on this rant for days. Too much oak, too much alcohol, too much fruit. In short, not Italian.

It takes a sour, orange wine with a tannic death-grip to finally elicit; "Now that's Barbera! You could drink this all day long," implying: and not fall off your chair and stain your teeth purple. To the untraveled Eskimo, I suppose, what Manolo Blahnik makes does not much resemble a shoe, either.

Touring Australia with an Italian provides ringside seats to the seismic shock of two wine cultures colliding. Australians might be closer to Europe in their drinking habits, but their winemaking ethos is as different as it gets.

European winemaking is an art, involving as much instinct and old family lore as science. Government regulations ensure the same disadvantages to all: in bad vintages, no one has recourse but to make bad wine, badly. To hell with absolutist, international standards of quality—they protest. It's about identity!

This is mystic mumbo-jumbo to the pragmatic Australian winemaker who packs a vast, viticultural bag of tricks and is not afraid to use it. Bad vintage? Simply import grapes from another region. The consistent, easy-drinking results may be pooh-poohed as „supermarket wine," but it conquered both England and America.

Lacking tradition, indifferent to appearances, Oz is free to do things that make Europe— even America—cringe. Like pioneering both screw-caps and casks (wine-in-a-box, to us) and so bringing yobbos and swillers of suds into the fold. Intuition, terroir, who needs them? Yellowtail, recently America's number one red import, sprung neither from a vineyard nor a vision, but from the desk of label designer Barbara Harkness, who calls her ready-to-go brand service, „Just Add Wine."

Somewhere between European pessimism ("Why start? I'll probably fail.") and American cockeyed optimism ("Every day in every way I'm getting closer to being a motivational speaker!") threads the Aussie worldview ("Yeah, hell exists, sod it.") As playwright David Williamson observes, "Most Australians… assume…that under the skin of a bastard lies an utter bastard." It's the sort of unshockable place where you can hear a little old lady observe that a cork is in "tight as a fish's ass."

As Americans know, the freedom that nurtures vigor also permits bad taste, a right I champion, even while pining for quaint, medieval towns, far from New World vulgarities.

Enrico, who lives in such a town, has a problem with vulgarity. Italians are more delicate, he insists. For instance, if you're staggering drunk, your problem is not too much wine, it's *non basta mangiare*—not eating enough. But *these* wines, oily, purple, practically sending up a plume of alcohol! No one could *mangiare basta*!

We do witness one Australian concession to subtlety: the obvious, overdone, American oak, responsible for wines so reeking of coconut and vanilla that even their über-fruit gets buried, is being replaced, in a mad stampede to...obvious, overdone French oak!

They say it wasn't until France put the kibosh on names like Champagne, Burgundy and Hermitage, that Australia really found her style. I'm not so sure it mattered. In this galaxy far, far away, comparisons with REAL French wine seem irrelevant.

The Barossa style, the most familiar to Americans, developed long ago when German immigrants gave up trying to make the neat, cool whites of their homeland and succumbed, like an English colonial officer "going native," to the wild imperative of the land, which was to produce big, red, juicy Shiraz.

That is by no means the only style. Australia has its share of small producers and subtle wine. There are cooler-climate Pinot Noirs and Rieslings, and quite a few Italian varieties; it's just that we see so few of them here. I hope that changes soon, because they're delicious wines, even if they don't taste like Europe. And why should they? Better to let a thousand grapevines bloom.

Ancient Region Opens to New World

Discover Phraxistan!

The tiny Republic of Phraxistan is poised to make its mark on the wine scene. Rich tradition, ancient vines, talented winemakers, none are particularly plentiful. Yet promise awaits in every direction: from the barren, rock-strewn, picnic areas of the East, to the lush, grassy plains, dotted with unexploded mines, in the West. From the abandoned steelworks in the North, to the "Lake Country" in the South, where lack of either lake or country attests to the lively Phraxic sense of humor plus a GPS malfunction.

For centuries, this deeply religious people reserved wine for sacred rituals, which occurred every hour on the half hour from Monday morning through midnight, Sunday. Thirsty tourists had to make do with a desultory bottle or two of overpriced, watery plonk. How things have changed! Now that wine is available worldwide!

One barrier to international acceptance is the Phraxic language, containing no vowels or consonants, only clicking,

"It adds the complexity of petrol without all that expensive aging."

spitting, snorting and, in the Northern dialect, blowing your nose. This makes the native grapes almost as tough to pronounce as they are to drink. The main red grape, often blended with Cabernet Sauvignon and Nyquil, is most closely rendered in the Roman alphabet as: q#!!*%>~&!.

Phraxic appellations are based on the easy-to-grasp uJjîtski system: 1uJjj indicates a wine made from unripe grapes, bitter, green and mouth-numbing, or, as Phraxans put it, "a food wine." 2uJjj is made from rotted grapes gathered off the ground of your neighbors' vineyards, while 3uJjj, the communist-era wine still widely produced and enjoyed today, is not actually made from grapes, but from used dry-cleaning fluid imported from Western democracies.

The mystery of how Phraxic grapes go from green to rotten without passing through a stage of ripeness will probably never be solved, due to the charming local tradition of *Hellwidit,* the pre-harvest festival where peasants throw down their tools and rush into cellars to polish off last year's wine, have sex and beat each other up.

To grasp the historical importance of wine in the Phraxic culture, one need only examine the numerous Roman-era amphorae depicting "Squirf," the popular ancient game of projectile vomiting, as well as pastoral scenes of young women washing stains out of togas while they curse.

Today, the budding wine industry is torn between the allure of the International Style and the authenticity of native grapes, although, thanks to traditional fertilizers rotting shellfish and road kill, the local terroir always prevails. Wines typically exhibit a signature smokiness, redolent not of French or American oak, but of black market Marlboroughs, chain-smoked by most cellar workers and generally extinguished in fermentation tanks. The acid level may seem high, but visitors soon find it perfect for cutting through the rich local cuisine of thistles, organ meat and lard, as well as for removing nail polish.

Whether it achieves consistent quality will depend in a large part on how willing vintners are to utilize modern technology. Vriîzor Xiîprit is typical of the new breed of boutique winemakers, the so-called *garagistes* and *outhousers.* "My Riesling develops in steel tanks," he says, indicating a '73 Yugo mounted on cinderblocks, "in this case, the carburetor. It adds the complexity of petrol without all that expensive aging." His reds undergo open-tank fermentation, usually in the bed of his pickup. If driving the rutted local roads doesn't keep the skins circulating during this critical period, then *battonage* is performed with a traditional local tool, the *vatvr*, Phraxic for "something lying around."

Some of the most notable wine comes from the relatively new appellation of Chr!#nbl^, where relaxed attitudes towards genetically modified crops, as well as the towering presence of a rusting, but still active nuclear power generator, result in enormous grapes, a fact not lost on Zwigliîp, whose thirteen fingers fly nimbly through the vines at pruning time. "Two bottles!" he grins, holding up a bowling ball sized grape. Much of this wine is sold in bulk to Western Europe where it is bottled under such labels, famous to customs impounders everywhere, as LaTour$_x$, Sassicaia$_x$ and Echezeaux$_x$.

Phraxic Pltzwiîn is reputedly the world's longest-aging wine. Indeed a trip through the vast network of caves that underlies towns that have not collapsed into it reveals thousands of bottles, easily twenty, sixty, even a hundred years old. These wines do not actually improve over time; it's just that no one wants to drink them.

If Phraxic wine does not share the exuberant fruit of the International Style, what it lacks in character it makes up in alcohol. While three-quarters of the wines in our tasting report scored less than 60 points, or "Gastric," the other quarter fared much better, being poured directly down the sink. Most of these wines are best drunk young—those over twenty seldom have the reflux muscles necessary for digesting them.

Few are aware that Phraxistan is the world's only producer of *lead* stemware. Factories were converted after Gwlmyiî Gwiîmp, local pop-psychologist and author of the best-selling *You Wouldn't Seem so Ugly if You Didn't Also Smell*, proclaimed crystal harmful to the self-esteem of the clumsy.

At the end of the day, what could compare with enjoying a glass of Phraxic Rütgüt, watching the sunset refracted through the smoke of a nearby vinyl factory, while soaking in the traditional pageantry of a Sanitation Workers Strike? As they say in Phraxistan, "M#^vstlx!"

Part IV: Drinking and Tasting

USING YOUR SENSES

Blind Faith

Playing tricks on your brain

When a press release arrived touting Riedel's new Blind-Blind tasting glass—fifty-nine dollars' worth of opaque-black, hand-blown crystal; designed to keep you in the dark about the wine it contains—I thought, "Ha! This is nothing but a wacky stunt to get the media's attention. Well, I, for one, am not falling for it!"

I don't think the glass fully addresses the blind-tasting issue, anyway. Why not add a lid, so you can't *smell* the wine either? And why fine crystal, which only serves to *enhance* the tasting experience? How about sourcing the glasses at the 7-11 coffee counter and calling them the Sommel-rofoam Series?

My inner wise-ass satisfied, I turned to the problem of objective tasting. The biggest challenge is shutting up your brain, so your palate can get a word in.

Brain: "!! Famous-Wine Alert !! Château Margaux, '59 ! "

Palate: "Yak drool."

A recent study scanned the brains of a group of trained sommeliers and a group of normal people, while they tasted wine. Both groups showed activity in the *amygdala*, the primitive pleasure center of the brain. But only the sommelier brains lit up in the emotionally- and intellectually-driven frontal cortex.

Apparently, the civilians were thinking, "Yum! Heap Plenty Good Wine!!" while the soms were thinking, "How do I maintain my supercilious and intimidating demeanor when I'm lying here in a paper gown with wires coming out of my head?"

The conclusion was that training and experience made it impossible for the sommeliers to leave their work at the office.

But even with your brain tied behind you, your own senses will betray you. Neuroscientists used to think that each sense went out and did its own investigative journalism and then reported back to the brain, whose job it was to turn the whole thing into a story, which would then be mislabeled by some headline writer who hadn't even read the damn thing. But now it turns out your senses are co-authors, capable of goading each other into downright libel.

Recent experiments illustrate this sensory con game at work:

Sound and Vision: one flash on a computer screen appears to be two, if it's accompanied by two beeps.

Sound and Touch: people who listen to raspy, scraping noises as they rub their hands together go looking for Lubriderm.

Vision and Taste: blue strawberries don't make you salivate like red ones do.

Vision and Touch: if your visual cortex is suppressed, your hands can't tell the difference between a hairbrush and a waffle iron.

Vision and Smell: cherry-*colored* wine does everything in its power to convince you that it *smells* like cherries. Reining in your imagination is no help, because in this case, you're not actually *visualizing* cherries. Instead, your eyes talk directly to your nose and tell it what to smell. If it knows what's good for it.

Even a well-trained sommelier can be fooled if you spike his Chardonnay with red food coloring. It's a pretty nasty way to play with someone's brain. But I'm used to it. When I was young and unformed, my father used to serve me pink and blue milk. He got it, he explained, from pink and blue cows. The idea was enchanting. Unfortunately, the tasting notes, in crayon, are illegible.

Clearly, the Blind-Blind glass could be a useful addition to the tasting lab, but I don't quite grasp the social value. If they handed me the black glass at a party I'd start looking around for the hit man. Fifty-nine dollars is a little steep, anyway, for this freelancer. But in order to bring the investigative truth to my readers, I have done the American thing and covered a glass of my own with duct tape. So far, all the wines I taste seem to share a silvery, metallic character.

Color Coding

Look & learn

You had a happy, healthy childhood in the sun; then developed an overbearing, graceless personality. But as you mature and lose your coarse edges, people will warm to your considerable charms. A crystal ball? No, I'm looking into a glass of wine, and I can see both its past and future.

Before the swirling and sniffing starts, skilled wine tasters already have some thirty percent of the info they need just by looking. Grape variety, growing area, weather, cellar techniques, age and how the wine will taste; all are written there for the observant sleuth. Learn some of these clues, and not only will you impress your friends and terrify your enemies; you just might get more from the whole wine-tasting experience.

The best way to judge color is to fill your glass halfway and tilt it sideways until the surface of the wine is an ellipse. Good lighting and a white background are essential.

"Grape variety, growing area, weather, cellar techniques, age and how the wine will taste; all are written there for the observant sleuth."

Red wines start out purple. Over the years they turn, like autumn leaves, from red, to brick to brown. The color also lightens with age. A faded, brownish wine, orange around the gills, has "retirement community" written all over it.

If it's inky enough to dip someone's pigtails in, it's "extracted." Extract refers to color, flavor, in short, everything that's not water. The more extracted the wine, the riper the grapes were at harvest. If you can't see the bottom of your glass, expect intense flavor.

You can tell something about grape variety by color as well. Petite Sirah, Syrah and Zinfandel are the purplest. The Cabernet family ranges from purple through cherry-red. Pinot Noir has a distinctly brownish cast that makes Burgundy lovers salivate on sight. Italian reds tend towards brick and orange.

Whites, conversely, pick up color with age. Colorless, pale green, silvery or pale straw tells you the wine is young, tart, refreshing and not super-fruity. Pinot Gris (or Grigio, same thing) is an example, as are Sancerre and White Bordeaux, both made from Sauvignon Blanc grapes.

As the color gets richer, so does the wine: malolactic, a secondary fermentation that removes green-apple flavors and replaces them with butter-cream, makes wine yellower. Fruit extraction does too. Oak aging, which adds body and vanilla-caramel flavors, produces canary-yellow tones. If your ideal Chardonnay is like a banana-split—thick, tropical and creamy—choose a deep-yellow wine.

Sweet, mature, dessert whites grow gold and then orange as they age. Late-harvest Riesling and Sauternes are two examples. Brown, though, is a bad thing. The wine is probably spoiled by oxidation.

If you see tiny bubbles, the wine's not quite done fermenting. This is a charming, youthful trait in a pale, young white. It's a fault in richer, older whites and a serious problem in reds.

Good wine glitters like a chrome bumper. A dull surface means the wine needs more acid and will taste rather flat. Don't worry if it's not altogether clear, though. Until quite recently, most wine was supposed to be as limpid as a swimming pool (not the municipal kind). These days, a good bit of it looks like the North Atlantic. What changed? What you're seeing is a trend towards unfiltered wine.

Filtering removes not just the unsightly bits of yeast, tannin and other flotsam, but also the flavors contained in this haze. A strong back-to-nature movement is propelling many winemakers to leave it alone.

It's a risky choice, though. Those old yeast cells are not always dead, and sometimes they get the notion to start fermenting again in the bottle. Especially when there's residual sugar to nosh on. Any number of other bacteria could be lurking there as well, fixing to spoil the wine. Filtering prevents all that.

What's better, then? Unfiltered and dangerous, or stable and predictable? As with so many wine choices, there are beauties in both categories. It's your choice.

If you know how to look, it's not hard to foresee the rich, intense, young Italian in your future. Meanwhile, if you can figure out how to predict where the stock market is going, let me know.

Treasure Hunt

Sniffing stereoisomers

"Burnished leather, lemon cream, marzipan and green tea," reads the description. The wine is also apparently "Long and lush with layers of papaya and mango emerging on the finish." *You* never taste things like that! You suspect the whole thing is a put-on; a ripe, calimyrna-figment of some blowhard's imagination.

Actually, it's not. There really is papaya in your wine glass, or at least its mirror-image twin—an odor molecule called a stereoisomer. A given glass might contain over 200 of these copycat chemicals, so it's not surprising we don't all pick up the same ones.

If wine critics notice things you don't, it's a matter of training. You, too, could learn to detect orange blossoms and cat pee. Should you bother? It's satisfying to have the sort of mental library that allows you to smell diesel and think "Aged Riesling from the Pfalz," although it's frustrating when the liquid in question is dripping from an eighteen-wheeler.

"You, too, could learn to detect orange blossoms and cat pee.
Should you bother?"

You could discover an extra dimension of pleasure, like when you finally find someone to translate the lyrics of that foreign song you've always loved. Although they generally turn out to be, "Oh, baby! Baby, baby, oh, oh!"

If you go hunting, give your nose a fighting chance. Swirl the wine thoroughly, and then plunge in deep enough to seal the glass with your face. Find your working nostril (it changes) and take a deep whiff. Take a sip and breath out through your nose to activate the retro-nasal route, another path to enlightenment. Exhale yet again after you've spit or swallowed.

Chances are you smell…something. But, what? Sometimes it's no more than an emotional vignette; e.g. the drawer in grandma's bedroom where she kept her big, scary bras. This is good! Wherever you are, write it down! Someday, that napkin may be worth something! Especially if the court needs a sample of your DNA.

The next step is to characterize your impression. Ask yourself: is it bright or dark? Tart or sweet? A whistle or a tuba? Pungent? Chemical? If you detect flowers or fruit, are they fresh or dried? What color do they smell like?

With as little as that, you can I.D. the thing for your own purposes. To me, the smell commonly known as bell pepper in Cabernet Sauvignon will forever be Creepy-Crawler, a brand of psychedelic plastic spider that could fascinate a bored, stoned teenager for hours. Or so they tell me. To other people, Cabernet smells like a Band-Aid. It need only resonate for you.

"Cheese fondue" was my instant reaction to a certain flavor I kept encountering in Germany. I haven't cleared up whether it was French bread, Gruyere, Kirshwasser or traumatic childhood dinners I was flashing on, but meanwhile the smell sends me reeling back to the Rheingau.

But if you want to describe wine to other people, you have to be more precise, and for that, nothing beats regularly smelling your way through the spice rack and the produce section. You can also haunt flower stores and perfume departments. When it gets to the part of the flavor wheel that includes wet mouse, though, you're on your own.

Is it really necessary to distinguish between, say, a white peach and a peach-colored peach? Yes! The first is much more impressive. When you get to this level, you also start smelling rocks, like a real wine pro. When you get so you can smell the difference between slate and granite, you'll know you've arrived! And so will the little people who live in your ear.

If you slam into a total block, it helps to know the sort of taster who can detect hazelnuts and violets and tactfully point them out to you. If this is a little more than you can stomach, it's acceptable to bluff. Riff on the "nuances of wild flugelberry on the mid-palate." No one will have the nerve to question you. And who knows, it might even show up in a wine column.

Body Check

Mouth sensations

"Broad-shouldered and thick," reads the note from one judge. "Firm and fleshy," says another. One contestant was deemed "a little awkward," while another had a "slim yet muscular frame." Finals of the Miss Aerobics America contest? No, just more excerpts from the weird world of wine ratings. If those evoked the swimsuit competition, how about these from the talent portion: "Goes for the gusto and pulls it off," "A bit lumbering, but full of personality," and "Manages to stay elegant and focused but...lacks follow-through." Believe it or not, these descriptions really do tell you something about wine, although you can't help picturing leering judges and bikinied babes when you read a comment like, "Ripe and easy....presented in a balanced package of wonderful seduction."

If you were to encounter an "Exuberant young red, bursting with aromas" would you allow it up on the couch?

And where could you safely store a wine that was likely to "sneak up on you, rather than hit you over the head?"

All of these are tasting notes from wine magazines, some of the raciest reading on my nightstand. What are they getting at?

Most of it refers to body. In the constant quest to make a potentially simple subject complex, we wine whackos like to address the body of wine separately from its soul. Body refers to viscosity or mouth-filling properties. One of the things that gets us going is that wine stimulates so many senses: color and clarity for sight, all kinds of tastes and smells, and I suppose you could stretch the point by including the fizz of champagne bubbles and the pop of cork as stimuli for the ears.

Body isn't the only tactile component in wine, but it's an easy one to appreciate. Imagine taking in a mouthful of 10-W-40. The way it feels when you roll it around your mouth epitomizes body. If oil or molasses is a ten, water is a one. Thick or heavy is not necessarily better; what's important is whether the viscosity is appropriate for the type of wine. You wouldn't send a supermodel to do a sumo wrestler's job. Once you understand body, and which wines you might expect to be more zaftig, it can add another dimension to your enjoyment.

Four things cause body:

1) Higher ratio of alcohol to water. (This also causes *legs* - the streams that flow down the side of the glass after swirling.)

2) The proportion of *extract*, i.e. everything that's not alcohol or water (which sometimes shows up as dregs in the bottom of your glass.)

3) Oak aging. Large molecules (oxymoron?) from the wood dissolve in the wine and make it thicker.

4) Sugar content: more sugar usually produces heavier body. (It certainly works that way for me.)

So, a dry, low-alcohol, white wine—a young Riesling for example—has a light body. So does a dry rosé. A well-oaked, well-aged—and therefore, more concentrated—Chardonnay has more body. So does a high-alcohol, inky-dark Zinfandel (that color is due to extracts). Very sweet dessert wines and fortified wines like port and sherry have the heaviest body of all.

I suppose if I had to write blurbs on fifty wines in one go, I'd skip "thin" and "thick" and go for "a lithe, dense structure," or "a sinewy frame." After all, even when you spit you're bound to absorb enough alcohol to unleash the pen. A note like: "the vintage peeks in on the firm finish" had to be written by a dirty old man. It's kind of reassuring, though, when even professional tasters are at a loss for words. Who can't relate to the review that begins simply, "Whoa! Very yummy..!"

Great Expectorations

Spitting is an art, too

You're pretty comfortable at a wine tasting. You toss around terms like "carbonic maceration" and "volatile acid." You avoid such social faux pas as surfacing from a deep sniff with red froth at the nostrils, or swirling your wine with centrifugal vigor clean across the room. You're ready to be a serious player. It's time to step up to the public trough, my friend, and spit.

Coming to terms with the *crachoir*, or spittoon, is a little like learning trapeze. Rule #1: never look down. Spend much time at the ocean? Know the exhilaration of sea spray in your face? Crachoir splashback is nothing like that. It's more like combining the intimacy of beagle slobber with the surprise of a plumbing backup.

You do not spit on the sly, the way you pick your nose. It's performed with proud public panache. But how? There are classes on vintages, regions, glasses and grapes, but no one

"It's time to step up to the public trough, my friend, and spit."

teaches proper spit-iquette. Out here, it's every man for himself.

And man, indeed, has the advantage. Equipped with his own, personal Super-Soaker, well-versed in snow calligraphy, he's profited from years of target practice while woman hits the saliva ceiling.

Spitting, for men, is a contest. From the Rhine to the Rhône, from Mendoza to Barossa, get two guys in a barrel cellar, and the undercurrent of one-spitsmanship is palpable.

I've seen them size up rows of barrels and nail a six-inch gap at three paces. I've marveled as neatly tapered arcs hit floor drains four feet distant, without splashing a drop. I've flinched as guided missiles find their target an inch from my toe. And they do all this pretending not to notice one another.

Hopefully they don't notice me either, because while they shoot jet streams through pinholes, I splatter my own shoes and wipe dribbles off my chin. If only I could spit like one of the boys! Oh, for the blowhole of the great white whale! For the insouciant pucker of the llama! Or, barring that, for the little gizmo on the Windex bottle that changes "spray" into "jet."

It's not bad in a dimly lit, mossy, Old World cave, with centuries of dirt and rotted wood on the floor. But those sterile, modern operations with their spanking, white floors make me skittish. No doubt they're hoping I'll lose my nerve and swallow and then I'll fall in love with their wine and my tasting notes the next morning will be in Sanskrit.

Because, of course, we spit for objectivity: to do the crime but not the time. Why isn't this copacetic at food events? If hawking wine is professional, then why is working your way through a Kit Kat bar by chewing, savoring and then spitting each bite considered an eating disorder?

Surely someone has to evaluate popcorn or sausages. How do they manage? I put the question to John Harrison, Official Taste Tester for Dreyer's Grand Ice Cream Company. His taste buds are insured for one million dollars. "I do not swallow the ice cream," he assures me. He calls his tasting process "The Three S's:" Swirl, Smack and Spit. (Smack is about "warming and aerating the sample and engaging the olfactory nerve.") Ice cream tasters, it turns out, look for the same things we do, like top notes, bouquet and aroma. His palate would not stay fresh if he swallowed, Harrison tells me, to say nothing of his physique. "As it is," he says, "I have a little paunch and cheek, but then who would trust a skinny ice cream taster?"

Well, for that matter, who would trust a wine taster who isn't a little looped? Marathon sessions with watermelon seeds have begun to sharpen my prowess at ptooie. One day I will be William Tell, Annie Oakley and Robin Hood rolled into one: The Sultan of Spit! And as such, I will dispense this advice: Always wear maroon.

GOOD & BAD

Good & Plenty

What defines "good wine?"

Did you think if you studied wine long enough you'd reach a point where everything you heard made sense? Hah! Never was there such a business for going all vague and romantic when you want to know something concrete. Bluff and confusion are rife at every level, and bold pronouncements can crumble when you ask for an explanation.

I know, because I routinely annoy the hell out of people by questioning everything I don't understand. If someone refers to "sweet tannins," I'll ask, "You mean sweet like sugary, or like nice? What do they feel like in your mouth? Are you sure it's tannin producing that effect, not something else?" I hound the poor guy until I get it.

Winemakers get the full Spanish Inquisition. Even vino-virgins are worth grilling. My writer-friend Bruce, who has sold more than one column based on how little he knows about wine, turns out to be hypersensitive to acid. He can't even tolerate German whites or Italian reds. His ability helped me learn the difference between the sting of acid and the sandblast of tannin.

Some issues can't find a consensus. I'm still working on what, exactly, "legs" tell you. And there's a certain earthy, barnyard smell I've heard described variously as phenols, Brettanomyces (an evil yeast), dirty barrels or simply *goût de terroir*, which is French for "*merde* happens."

Is there room on this shaky platform for an objective definition of "good wine?" There are sweet wines and dry, gooey and bracing, cheap and dear, let alone personal preferences. Given all that, are there a few universal traits all good wine should show?

Yes, I say, after hundreds of interviews and thousands of tastes. Here then, in more or less concrete terms, are the standards I hold every wine to, regardless of pedigree or price.

Beauty: whether inky or pale, the fading orange of old Bordeaux or the vibrant, buttery yellow of California Chardonnay, good wine should be eye candy.

Nose: if it needs dinner and a movie to come around, you're working too hard. The aroma should jump right out of the glass and seduce you. Too shy can lose the sale right here.

Fruit: I want to taste it. Connoisseurs of musty old Bordeaux, be damned. I don't require a K.O. punch, although that's one style. But to a wine that tastes only of barrels, yeast or bottle-age I say, "Where's the beef?"

Midpalate: For years I thought this referred to a sort of dental G-spot, a place I was supposed to have but I didn't know where. Turns out it's what you taste after the initial rush subsides. Some wines build like a tsunami only to die before they hit the beach. Good wine you can surf in to shore. GREAT wine continues to evolve, in succeeding waves of aromas and sensations.

Balance: If one aspect sticks out to where you want to whack it like a mole, the wine is out of balance. Overwhelming coconut and vanilla from oak can do this. So can burning alcohol, or acid that does a Rembrandt on your teeth. Some wines are gawky adolescents but smooth out as they mature. Baby Cabernet, for instance, can nestle for years in a cocoon of tannin before emerging in all its splendor. You might not recognize that puckering mouthful as a diamond in the rough, but at least you can safely say it's not very good to drink NOW.

Finish: What remains after spitting or swallowing. You shouldn't feel violated, spackled or on fire. A good finish plays out like your first French kiss from a long-term, unrequited crush. Not like the slobber of Uncle Henry when he's been hitting the eggnog.

I'll confess, I've fallen for some wines that didn't measure up to all of this. But they needed something pretty powerful to compensate. I seem to have drifted into poetry in spite of myself. But, I swear, there's solid science behind every stanza.

Waiter, There's a Horse in My Wine

Gross things in good wine

"Bacon fat, game and the leather on the well-worn back seat of an old Jag." "Dried apricot, Band-Aid and geranium." Which is the bad wine review?

We like some pretty weird things in wine. Remember sliding that first, slimy oyster down your throat, after being told it was...alive? That first sip of scotch? Neither came naturally. You had to be introduced. By the same token, someone has to explain to the wine beginner why the scent of horse manure is shunned, while the tang of cat pee is prized.

Beauty often walks a tightrope. The trick is not falling into bland on one side, or disgusting, on the other. Of course, not everyone strings their wire in the same spot.

Some wines are made by assembly line; unflawed, perfect and perfectly boring. Others are less predictable, sometimes showing the little quirks that make wine lovers shiver with excitement.

Earth, usually the mark of a European wine, can add that frisson. In Burgundy, that means leaves rotting on the forest floor. It could also be rich, loamy compost. Or the dusty smell of bone-dry corrals and wind over the barren prairie. Oh, wait, that's my lawn.

Do you like your Riesling regular or unleaded? This grape is famous for developing aromas of diesel, although some people prefer to call it honeycomb, another waxy, petrol product. Cat pee shows up commonly in Sauvignon Blanc, especially in the twangy, New Zealand variety.

These are good things. A bad one is the cork-born contaminant, TCA, usually described as musty, dank basement, wet cardboard, or dirty gym socks.

If your nose tingles from lively acid or from the black pepper odors in wines like Syrah and Grüner Veltliner, that's lovely. If it prickles from sulfur dioxide, like when you smell a burnt match, or from the vinegary sting of volatile acidity, that's a problem.

Let's recap:

Damp Forest: good / **Damp Cellar:** bad.

Garage: good / **Locker Room:** bad.

Tingle: good / **Prickle:** bad.

How's a neophyte to know?

Often good and bad are the same chemical at work, in different concentrations. A small amount of ethyl phenol gives left-bank Bordeaux its sophisticated, mens-club aroma of tobacco and new saddle leather. Too much, and you get sweaty saddle and the horse it rode in on.

Since a hint of this can garner very high ratings, winemakers sit around figuring out how to encourage it without letting the responsible yeast and bacteria get out of hand and take over the winery.

The "correct" amount is purely subjective. Some people like more funk in their wine than others. It tends to be a European taste.

Which begs the question: do we expect, tolerate, even like funky stuff in wine simply because for so long it couldn't be prevented? Should wine, ideally, be totally clean, tasting only of fruit?

Might as well ask if blue cheese should be bleached, or if jerky should be re-hydrated. Lots of food that began as an accident ended up a delicacy.

Once you've been introduced to the gross things in good wine, you can decide for yourself what's a fault and what's a beauty mark. The only fault we can all agree upon—by far the worst—is the one where the cork is out of the bottle and there appears to be no wine inside.

When Good Wines Go Bad

Detecting faults

The wine came highly recommended, but it smells like horse-sweat and tastes like wet ashes. Is there something wrong with it, or are you just not sophisticated enough to appreciate Château de Phlegm '89?

With wine, there's a wiggly line between a fault and a virtue. For instance, the smells of diesel fuel, cat-pee and Old MacDonald's farm sound like faults, yet they are accepted, even prized as expressions of *terroir* in Alsace Riesling, Sancerre and Burgundy, respectively. The components in the first paragraph are not unwelcome in a Rhône-style Syrah.

There are, however, a few official faults, which are handy to know about if you're feeling gypped. While sending wine back simply because you didn't like it will not help your popularity rating, you are quite within your rights returning wine that's truly gone bad.

Here are some signs, then, that your wine has been spoiled by bacteria, heat, cork taint or exposure to air, the big four culprits.

Seal: If the seal is shot, so is the wine. A cork that's crumbly, dry or comes out too easily is not doing its job. If it's wet *all the way through* it's no doubt leaking air as well as wine. These are the things to check for when the waiter hands you the cork. Don't worry if the cork has white crystals on the bottom or mold on the top.

A fill-level lower than the top of the bottle's shoulder suggests an evaporation problem. This air space is known as *ullage*, as in "ullage you have this bottle for $4.99."

Looks: Hazy, oily, and cloudy are bad. So are strange things floating around (unless they are cork that you knocked in there). Unfiltered wine, which we're seeing a lot more of, is not crystal clear, but at least the surface should reflect light. If a red or white wine looks strangely brown or orange, it might be oxidized or over the hill.

Smell: Musty and stale are bad. The smell of wet cardboard spells trouble with a capital T that that stands for 2,4,6-Trichloroanisole, or cork taint. If it smells like sherry, but it's not, the wine is *cooked*, or oxidized.

Taste: Sour and tasteless are both faults. Fizzy (in a supposedly still wine) is a sign of childish gaiety in young whites, but a serious fault in reds and older wines. Immature wine, in all its tannic nastiness, is only a timing fault, not a wine fault. You weren't so pleasant as a teenager, either.

Very old wines cannot be judged by these rules. Engage the services of a qualified Sherpa for your first foray into them, or risk certain disappointment.

If you decide to bring or send a flawed bottle back, chances are they'll accommodate you. Whimpering helps. To grease the skids, as four out of five coaches once said, the best defense is a good offense and vice versa. I.e., make a habit of engaging the merchant or sommelier *before* you choose wine, and you've got a much better chance at restitution. Ask what an unfamiliar bottle is supposed to taste like. Caveat emptor: I've heard some pretty strange answers to customers' questions at big discount stores. If it's advice you want, go to a specialty wine shop.

If you can't find a fault, but you still don't like it, remember, in wine, one man's nectar is another man's Tidy Bowl. Just chalk it up to experience.

Unleaded

Science & poetry of tasting notes

The oyster tasting did it. I love teaching people the joys of analyzing wine. My friend Peter, however, cannot drink alcohol, so we tried the process on other things, like orange juice, Thai duck soup and oysters. It's a mistake to scrutinize oysters that carefully. After the third time writing "slimy, fishy," I decided enough was enough. I was going to find some non-alcoholic wine.

De-alcoholized wine is not just fancy fruit juice. "Noble" grapes, the likes of Chardonnay and Merlot are fermented, aged—often in oak—filtered and fined, just like the real thing. Only then is the alcohol removed.

One method is the "spinning cone." The wine spins until it becomes a film; then the aroma and flavor compounds are removed and safeguarded. The remaining liquid is heated repeatedly until all the alcohol is gone. Then the two are reunited.

"Here are his tasting notes. Did I mention he's a poet?"

Another method is cold filtration. The wine is repeatedly pressed through a filter so fine that only alcohol and water, the smallest molecules, go through, leaving a syrupy residue behind. This concentrate is then re-hydrated to its original strength. Proponents of both processes claim they retain both the delicate flavors and mouth-feel of the original wine.

I thought I knew about wine snobbery. Hah! "You're looking for *what*?" said my pals in the industry, "Why even bother? Alcohol is a natural part of wine. Without it..." they made a face, "you might as well drink...Kool-Aid."

Why bother indeed? Because wine is for sharing. What's the fun of swirling, swishing, sloshing and yakking if my friends can't join in? Sure, alcohol adds flavor and body, and I'm not knocking the buzz. But it's not what I read and write and rave about. The beauty of wine is its complexity. Do my teetotalling friends have to miss all the fun?

My contacts tried to head me off with low-test beer. Indeed, there are some good ones, but beer is prose, while wine is poetry. Martinelli's sparkling cider? Sorry, that's just Mott's on CO_2.

An Internet search turned up little. Apparently, only three companies are big enough to risk a non-alcoholic brand. There's Sutter Home's Fré, Inglenook's St. Regis Reserve, and J. Lohr's Ariel.

Peter is a sophisticated, well-read, world-traveler; the sort of guy that would know a lot about wine if he could drink it. Did I mention he's a poet? I invited him to taste with me—his first time. Here are our notes.

Flight 1: Sparkling Wines
Ariel Brut Cuvée

Me: Off-dry, tiny bubbles, white flowers and creamy custard.

Peter: You're fifteen years old, it's November, you're walking home through an orchard of frozen apples, your feet are wet, and the girl you took to the movies didn't kiss you.

Fré Brut

Me: Pungent fruit, lively acid, salty, long finish.

Peter: A steel hull bumping against a dock-piling in a stiff wind.

Flight 2: Chardonnay

Fré Chardonnay 2000

Together: Odd, rotting fruit and something waxy, Janitor-in-a-Drum? Grape juice in a box. Late orange-peel attack, salty.

Ariel Chardonnay 2001

Me: Smoke, tobacco–

Peter: –smelled through an old, metallic screen door.

Me: Supple acid, grapey, floral, clean finish.

Peter: A flock of pelicans landing on the ocean.

Inglenook St. Regis Reserve Chardonnay

Me: Strong varietal character, tobacco and…wet underpants? Lively acid, salty, long spicy finish. *Peter:* Monkey house at zoo. Hitting a softball into the pine trees.

Flight 3: Merlot and Cabernet Sauvignon

Fré 2002 Merlot

Me: Intense cherry, candy apple and cinnamon, with lingering grape tannins.

Peter: Blue velvet; smoking a pipe in a leather chair.

Ariel 1999 Cabernet Sauvignon

Me: Overpowering toasted American oak, structured tannins, cherry cola.

Peter: Creosote-soaked railroad tracks, vanishing into the horizon.

Inglenook St. Regis Reserve Cabernet

Me: Dry earth, cedar, licorice and black pepper with a burst of black cherry and a long, spicy finish.

Peter: A thin, dusty, old carnival worker, chewing gum in the sun.

Inglenook took honors in the end, also the best match for slightly stale club crackers. Ariel was a close second. Many had an odd saltiness, perhaps a byproduct of the process.

Sure, they could be better, but we genuinely liked them. Comparing them to real wine is beside the point. For a certain segment of people, wine is simply not on the menu. The relevant comparison is to the alternatives.

Peter says he will definitely buy more. If you, too, must abstain, should you bother with non-alcoholic wine? Absolutely. Note to all the snoots who tried to dissuade me: Grow up!

RESTAURANT ISSUES

Sommelier Bares All!

Inside skinny on the man in white

It's a chilling moment. You've perused the wine list to page twenty-eight—middleweight Estonian Malbecs—when you sense a presence lurking by your chair. Do not ask for whom the sommelier calls; he calls for thee. Sleek and superior, he waits, while you blither. Quick, think of something smart to order!

Relax. Just for you, I parachuted behind enemy lines and captured a live sommelier. When I threatened to take his corkscrew, things got ugly and he decided to talk. He was misunderstood, he said. And his story unfolded.

The sommelier, he told me, evolved from the English butler, a robotic creature whose two main duties were to tend the wine cellar and terrify guests. But that vestigial snootiness is dying out. Today's sommelier is often young and enthusiastic. He's here to help, not humiliate.

"Do not ask for whom the sommelier calls; he calls for thee."

Sensing my skepticism, the captive asked, "How much do you know about the internal combustion engine?" Um... "Do you want to take the time to learn? Of course not! You want to walk onto a car lot and say, 'I need a good car. Don't screw me.' Same thing with wine. As sommeliers, we do the homework for you. Trust us. Use us."

"But how can we trust you," I asked, "when you're sneering at us? What are you guys actually thinking?"

"We don't judge you by your wallet," he replied, "possibly the reverse. A $200 Bordeaux or Napa Cabernet is an insurance premium on quality: safe, expensive and...BORING! We spend all this time putting together a creative wine list. Explore it! We're as intrigued by the exciting new find, the great *deal*, as you are.

"Don't try to impress us with your encyclopedic knowledge of vintages in the Côte de Beaune. But we like talking wine, so do ask questions. If you must show off a little, you could start with, 'Considering the unfortunate precipitation during the '92 harvest in the Haut-Médoc, how's the Château Ungepatch drinking?' But we'd much prefer, 'I once had a Chianti and it tasted like salad dressing. Are they all like that?'

"Our ideal customer? An honest one: 'I can't spend more than thirty dollars, it needs to go with everyone's dinner, and I hate red,' is something we can sink our teeth into. Or an adventurous one: 'Make me feel like I'm at the bullfights in Rioja!' That will win you a sommelier friend for life.

"Reading a table is an art. Romantic dinner à deux? Make the guy look suave in front of his date. High-roller clients being schmoozed? Don't let the host come across cheap. The woman's reading the wine list? Don't, for God's sake, insult her by assuming the man will order. And when you make recommendations, be on the lookout for the involuntary jolt that runs through the customer's body when you reach his price ceiling.

"It's all very well to hear, 'My wife and I fell in love over a zingy little white number at a chalet in the Alps. Can you find us something like that?' Sure we can, but minus the original moment of sizzle, our excellent choice might very well fizzle."

I asked what was up with the silver ashtray hanging around his neck. "The *tastevin*," he told me, "had facets that reflected light, for tasting wine in a candlelit cellar." But does it serve any purpose today, in a restaurant? He hesitated. "I have difficulty discerning particulars without more appropriate glassware." (Sometimes they can't help talking like that.) Then he sighed. "I've tried using the damn thing; I've really tried, for twelve-plus years...

"Next time a sommelier psyches you out," he concluded as I returned him to his cellar, "just remember: no matter how much you spend, what you're getting is still four and a half glasses of grape juice."

Sign Language

Translating the wine list

At the Airport Grill, where my dad used to take us for a hamburger in the '60s, the bathroom choice was "Pilots" or "Stewardesses." A slam-dunk lawsuit today, still, you knew where you stood (or sat, if you were a stewardess.) It certainly beats having to decide if you're a Buoy or a Gull, a Turtle or a Tortoise, or which of the odd silhouettes most resembles you and your clothing. Easier, too, than my neighborhood hangout, Mel's, where the triple choice of Men, Women and Ladies requires more reflection than I'm usually in the mood for.

A too-cute wine list scratches the same blackboard. I applaud restaurants for the effort, but headings like "Grills, Thrills and Wild Things," "Cutting Edge," and "Silver Linings," raise more questions than they answer.

Attempting to describe wine makes sense if you share a common language. Alas, many terms mean one thing on wine lists, another to professional tasters and a third to the average diner. Let's decode some common ones.

243

"I can't spend more than thirty dollars, it needs to go with everyone's dinner, and I hate red."

Dry: Refers to sugar, or lack of it. Does *not* mean mouth puckering, rough, tooth coating or bitter. Those are the work of tannins and acids. Dry wine can be smooth as silk. High-alcohol wine, like Viognier or Zinfandel, sometimes *seems* sweet, even with little or no sugar. Taste a little rubbing alcohol and you'll see.

Rich: If they made Shiraz-flavored Kool-Aid and you used seven packets for one pitcher, you'd have rich. Also known as concentrated or extracted, it means more color and flavor.

Fruity: Does *not* mean sweet. Arguably, all wine should be fruity—it's made from fruit, for heaven's sake! If you smell peach, pineapple, blackberry, and, yes, even grape, the wine is fruity. (If you pick up gooseberry, you're faking it. Gooseberries are a hoax perpetuated by wine critics, and do not, in fact, exist. Quince and bramble, two other common wine descriptors, do exist, but no one really knows what are.) On a wine list, fruity usually means simple: you taste the fruit and nothing but the fruit.

Floral: Smells like perfume, flowers, or the soap in the guest bathroom that everyone's afraid to unwrap.

Spicy: Exotic. Can refer to anything in the spice rack. Gewürztraminer is always described as spicy because, a) that's what Gewürz means and b) there aren't any other things that smell like it. Spicy in a Syrah means cinnamon and black-pepper-up-your-nose.

Body: A tactile thing: the glop factor. Light-bodied is skim milk or water. Full-bodied is heavy cream or honey.

Big! Huge! Blockbuster! A Monster!: Three possible meanings. With California Zinfandel, it refers to how your head will feel the next morning; that is, the wine packs a punch. In the case of Cabernet or Barolo, it means tannins like a three-day-old beard. Either the wine is too young, or you're meant to tough it out, saying things like, "Now THERE'S a wine!" Applied to other reds, it means super-rich and full-bodied. Beware; when it comes to food, blockbuster wines are about as friendly as a Sumo wrestler with diaper rash.

Soft: This term sells oceans of Merlot every year. It means not enough acid or tannin to last, refresh or excite. Lemonade without the lemons. No complexity, nothing that would tax your brain. It's a plot, can't you see?? They think you're too lowbrow to appreciate anything better than Pablum. They want to turn you into pod people! Forget soft wine! Get out of that ghetto, man! Make like an infinitive and split!

If you follow these guidelines and still aren't crazy about the wine they bring, give it a chance with your meal. Underwhelming sipping-wine can make beautiful music with food. But go easy on it, or you could find yourself dancing up and down in front of two doors, trying to figure out whether you're a Porpoise or a Dolphin.

Half Time

Half the bottle, twice the fun

In the quest to retain my girlish figure, I have a rule: never eat for the sake of the food. The fact that last night's baked ziti is alone in the dark refrigerator, wailing to be eaten, doesn't oblige you to come to its rescue. The garbage pail can handle the job just fine. I have trouble, though, applying this strategy to wine. Maybe it's the frightening markup some restaurants charge. Perhaps it's knowing that the winemaker put just a tad more skill and effort into the bottle than I did into the ziti. Either way, a wine is a terrible thing to waste.

That means if an unfinished bottle goes in the fridge, I'm morally bound to drink it the next night before it spoils. It means that while dining out, even on top of an aperitif or two, I *must* not leave until the wine bottle is empty. Never mind the impending drive home and the inevitable hangover.

The dilemma: you love fine wine, you hate wasting money, but you just can't drink like you used to.

The solution: the half-bottle. A European institution, the half-bottle concept is picking up steam in this country. Rumor has it poised to be the Next Big Trend.

A smashing idea it is. Think of the problems solved. You're out to dinner with one of those "Wine's first duty is to be red and damn the Pad Thai noodles!" types, and you had your heart set on Grüner Veltliner. Your choices are: duke it out, give in, or order from the by-the-glass menu, which, incidentally, has come a long way from the desultory days of the "house" brand.

But with half-bottles an option, you can sip your white, watch your companion try and stoke firecracker shrimp with Barolo, and each be responsible for only the equivalent of two glasses. If the two of you are more compatible, wine-wise, you might want to share a Sancerre with salad, followed by a Cab with the prime rib. Get a half-bottle of each and nothing goes to waste.

Not that this has ever happened to anybody, but say you were the brilliant one who chose the wine and it turns out tasting like bilge water, only you don't want to admit it, and besides, the waiter insists that it's "correct for its type." Well, then, hey, the smaller the bottle, the shorter the humiliation.

Somewhere between a three-martini power-fest and a low-carb energy bar on the Stairmaster lies the civilized lunch; a perfect time for the half-bottle. Returns you to the office in the ultimate, productive state: mellow but not sloshed.

A half-bottle is just the thing for the business traveler dining alone, trying to look romantic instead of pathetic. Or, for one of those mixed marriages between a wine-lover and someone with more rational uses for excess money.

As that pig-in-the-python demographic, the baby boomers, age, their days of slamming back Long Island ice tea and tequila Jell-O shots are fading. They're drinking fine wine, and not to get snockered. They may fill their SUVs with twelve-packs of cheerios and toilet paper from Bob's Bulky Bunker, but their wine buying is more selective. The industry will do well to pay attention. Half-bottles are also a way for wineries to take a little of the intimidation factor out of ordering a very pricey wine, thereby exposing more consumers to more choices. Everyone wins.

Ounce for ounce, you may pay a little more, since bottling, corking and labeling are a fixed cost regardless of bottle size. But perhaps it's time to start drinking less but drinking better, as opposed to the Sir Edmund Hillary approach of finishing wine simply because it's there.

Sedimental Journey

Decanting: pretension or necessity?

Omar Khayyam realized that wine was more than just a drink in a bottle after the failure of his first draft, "A loaf of bread, some frozen orange juice, and thou." Wine is holy, hence surrounded by rites both sacred and profane. Which is which? How do you tell the useful from the pretentious? The swirling from the cork-sniffing? Surely, you'd think, the second category describes decanting.

But you'd be wrong. Besides selling expensive crystal and impressing people, decanting really improves certain wines. Like diapers, it's for the very young and the very old.

Some immature reds are harsh, tannic and sullen. Years of slow exposure to oxygen in the bottle will help them grow up, mow the lawn and get a 401(K) plan. But if you want to drink now, and your wine has a scraggly goatee and waist/pants placement issues, oxygen is the Marine drill sergeant you need for an attitude adjustment.

Aerate that puppy by letting it splash vigorously into a decanter, first taking the safety precaution of wearing proper eye protection and a maroon sweater. Then let it sit and pant for an hour. Despite what many restaurants think, wine can no more "breathe" through the neck of an uncorked bottle than you can suck a pork chop through a straw.

Alternatively, you can buy a little wand that churns up the wine in your glass for the same effect, very useful if you're a PR firm looking for a new gizmo to bear the company logo.

To appreciate the effects of oxygen, try this fun experiment: get two bottles of the same wine and decant one. An hour later, open the second. Taste both. Rinse. Repeat.

Elderly wines need decanting because, in wine parlance, they "throw a sediment," a surprisingly athletic way of saying that the tartaric acid crystals and color pigments separate and sink to the bottom of the bottle with the velocity of a speeding glacier.

You do not want to drink this sludge, although it's crunchy and interesting to taste to those of us stuck in the developmental stage of learning about the world around us by putting it in our mouth.

The procedure, this time, is slightly different. A day or two before drinking, shake the bottle gently to remove sediment encrusted on its sides, and stand it upright. At drinking time, pour the wine slowly and continuously into the decanter, watching the bottleneck carefully for a ribbon of sediment. When it appears, stop pouring. Do not play chicken with this stuff.

If you didn't plan ahead, and the bottle's still resting, keep it that way. Uncork it lying down (the bottle, not you) and pour from that position (OK, you can if you want). That's what waiters are doing when they pour wine from a basket.

For the über-suave, SO over the need to impress, the same thing can be accomplished with a coffee filter and a funnel.

I have been known to decant into 7-11 Big Gulp cups (the plastic collector's edition of course) but the fun thing about real decanters is that you can go crazy with cut crystal, etched glass, and colors, all the things a wine glass shouldn't be.

Shape and size matter. You need room for the contents of a whole bottle without the surface of the wine rising higher than the widest point of the decanter. Above that, you don't get enough surface area in contact with air. (The flared contours of the Big Gulp preclude this problem.)

For what it's worth, the same holds true for fish bowls: overfill and you'll suffocate the guppies. Also, they seem to prefer water to wine.

SERVING & DRINKING

Glazed and Confused

The Riedel mystique

Part I

I'm coming down off a gnarly dishwashing episode. Handling my four Riedel wine glasses, large as cabbages and ephemeral as spider-webs, gets me so jumpy that sometimes I'd rather just get it over with and smash them to smithereens sooner rather than later.

I got them at a Riedel tasting, an event where they demonstrate Austrian crystal-maker Georg Riedel's theory that the shape of the glass affects the taste of the wine. The Rolls-Royce of wine paraphernalia, Riedel glasses (pronounced REE-dle), at up to ninety bucks a pop, have won over such wine deities as the Roberts: Parker and Mondavi.

But do they deliver? The Riedel tasting I attended was more Tupperware party than physics class. The idea seemed to be: get them drinking, get them laughing, toss in some science, and sell, sell, sell!

The tongue map, which divides your taste buds into zones for salt, sweet, bitter and sour, is at the heart of the theory. Incidentally, studies today call the tongue map a myth, but no matter, the idea is that a glass that directs a very narrow flow of wine to the tip of the tongue will emphasize sweetness in an austere wine. With the right shape, they say, you can direct a young Bordeaux away from your tannin sensors, or a buttery Chardonnay toward your acid receptors. You need a cut rim to achieve this; the rolled rim on cheaper glasses might as well direct wine into your ear for all the good it does you.

We tasted four wines, each from its "correct" glass, then from different shapes in the Riedel lineup, and last from what they called the "joker" glass. This squat, roll-rimmed object of derision is known to wine pros as the International Standard Tasting Glass.

Like a Baptist congregation, the people around me were seeing the light, praising the Cabernet in the Cab glass, damning it in the Pinot Noir glass. I, alone, was not saved. But maybe I'm just crabby—I thought, since I seem to be the only one spitting instead of swallowing after "initiating flow," as the Riedel people put it.

So, I went home and set up my own tasting. Four wines, four Riedel glasses. Plus two of my own—very thin, well-shaped, $3.98 at the outlet mall—and one joker glass. I tasted blindfold, concentrated hard and took copious notes. Result? Nada. Niente. Zip. OK, one difference. The enormous bowl and small opening on a couple of the Riedels did the best job of concentrating the aroma and bouquet of the Pinot Noir. That was it.

I still have questions. This tongue-flow business is about first impressions. But a mouthful of wine is a movie, not a snapshot; sensations unfold slowly, but eventually you get them all, no matter what came first. And why would you want to "correct" the acidity in a crisp, green-apply Riesling, or the creaminess in a malolactic Chardonnay? Moreover, if shape is so crucial that there's one glass for Bordeaux and another for Bordeaux *Grand Cru*, then how can all seven of the Champagne shapes they offer be correct?

None of this is to say they're not exquisite glasses. Like writing with a really fine pen, or swinging just the right golf club, holding a Riedel just feels good. Lead crystal, they tell me, has a rougher surface than glass, so more wine sticks to it when you swirl and there's more to smell. Speaking of swirling, some of the odder shapes are serious fun to swirl. You can work up a tornado reminiscent of the whirling vortex of a good old-fashioned, high-flush toilet.

While I'm not a convert on the shape issue, I'm certainly open if a Riedel guru would like to take another stab at enlightening me. Meanwhile, maybe it's just a case of reverse snobbery, but Shamu-sized bowls just strike me as pretentious. And as for the handling and breakage factor, well, until I either grow up or calm down, I think I'll stick with the joker.

Part II

A few weeks after that article runs, I get a call from a woman who says, "I'm with the Riedel Company." I expect her next words to be, "and you are SO busted!"

In fact, it's a summons from President Georg Riedel, himself. He wants a word with me. How good a taster am I? Where do I come off dissing the tongue-map, a central part of the Riedel theory? He is flying me to Chicago to meet with him. I WILL see the light.

Standing my ground presents a challenge when we meet, as I'm hit by gale-force Euro-Aristo charm. Riedel is impeccably dressed, speaks with a soft Austrian accent and, oh! those steely-blue eyes. I am dancing across a moonlit terrace with Captain Von Trapp. You will never be a nun, Maria. He says he hasn't seen the movie.

First stop: a tasting for forty people in a vaulted cellar, once a speakeasy. In fact, if the prohibition-era posters lining the walls have it right, Al Capone was killed here a few times before he died for good of tax evasion. Oddly, bones protrude from the brick walls. "See, the cannibals have been here," Riedel observes, "The people who didn't finish their wine were eaten."

I recognize the placemats, with three circles for the Riedel glasses and two for their lousy, stupid, laughable competitors. I notice that the tongue map is gone.

"I'm going to ask the ladies if I may take off my jacket," Riedel begins, detonating a mass female swoon. We taste Cabernet, Pinot Noir and Chardonnay from both sets of glasses. Riedel reels the audience in and out like a swordfisherman. A little science here, a story there, a tasting exercise, a joke; the rhythm is masterful.

Riedel glasses are shaped to emphasize different qualities in each wine. They affect not only the smell, but the taste as well, by directing wine to specific parts of your mouth. Or so they say. My quarrel has been that no matter what you taste first, the other components reveal themselves anyway in a matter of seconds. Besides, I can't taste the difference.

When I tap my glass it quivers like something alive and nervous and makes a sound like a temple bell. The cut rim is so thin and crisp that I want to bite off a piece and crunch it between my teeth. "Drinking is sensuous," says Riedel. "Really everything is sensuous."

I want so much to believe. I keep pouring wine from glass to glass, comparing. Converts cry out around me. I am the leper, the one sentient being in a sea of hypnosis.

Later that night, Riedel takes me to dinner. We eat tiny, exquisite things served in bamboo boxes and washed down with Burgundy and Austrian Riesling. The crystal is Riedel, the wine is remarkable, but is it...*different*?

Designing glasses, Riedel says, is trial and error. He'll try twenty shapes. He consults experts. Rhône winemakers, for example, helped build the Syrah glass. When tequila makers disagreed with him on a design—he wanted to emphasize aromatics over alcohol—he deferred to their judgment. As viticulture technology ping-pongs between Old World and New, ever ratcheting up the quality of wine, he invents new shapes to suit.

"What happened to the tongue map?" I ask. It's the only time I don't get a straight answer and I feel smug.

A reconnaissance mission at the Four Seasons bar turns up no Riedel stemware, so we suffer through a couple of single-malts in tumblers. I have a vision of Riedel standing over a bathroom sink, designing the perfect toothbrush glass. One that sends streams of water directly to the plaque deposits between your molars when you rinse.

Then I catch those eyes again. My skeptical side has temporarily left the building. At this moment, correct shape or not, my glass runneth over.

Raise Up High the Auction Paddle

Drinking songs for America

It was embarrassing. The Germans led us in a stein-draining rendition of "Ein Prosit," and the French had us chanting "Et glou! Et glou!" as we glou-gloued down our second glass. The Swedes and Italians serenaded us through shots of grappa and schnapps. But now it was the Americans' turn and damned if we could come up with a drinking song.

We were twenty wine journalists from around the world, wrapping up a week of tasting in Germany. A few of the locals at the little inn in the Rheingau joined in as our last supper evolved into a toast-a-thon; each country offering up its favorite down-the-hatch ditty. They had dozens to choose from and seemed to know every word. We Americans looked blankly at each other. Our memory of beer-swilling games in the "Hi, Bob" tradition was dim. "A Hundred Bottles..." was far too many to inflict on friends, and really more road-trip tranquilizer than toast.

"The Star Spangled Banner swiped its tune from a Revolutionary War-era drinking song."

The Europeans tried to help us. Surely there was a song, even if not drink-specific, that all Americans knew. The kind that would bring a Yankee restaurant to its feet when they heard the first few bars? We couldn't think of any. "Row, Row, Row Your Boat" had the ubiquity, but not exactly the raunchy abandon required. As for the national anthem, no one— especially not those pre-game hot-doggers who want to turn it into a half-hour scat-fest—can sing it.

How did we get into this sorry state: a country with no drinking songs? We had no shortage of taverns, colleges and brothels, all the usual breeding grounds. The truth is, we *did* have songs, once. In fact the "Star Spangled Banner" (a verse of which, dear ballpark auditioners, ought to take no more than a minute) swiped its tune from a Revolutionary War-era drinking song. "To Anacreon in Heaven" was the lofty title, and like all good songs of the genre it celebrated both wine and sex, exhorting the listener to "twine the myrtle of Venus with Bacchus's vine."

Prohibition might have been the culprit. Roaring-twenties bootleggers were in the business of keeping quiet. "Joe sent me" didn't much lend itself to musical treatment. And by the time the Eighteenth was repealed, the old drinking songs had been forgotten.

While Europeans dive heart and soul into a meal, we Americans tiptoe through the gastronomical tulips of guilt, avoiding either bread or butter according to the diet fad we're following, pretending we don't want dessert, and skipping the post-prandial *digestif* because we have to get up in the morning and go to work. We simply have no time to wallow around in *gemütlichkeit*. What a shame! The goal of college drinking games may be to get sloshed and quick, but the grown-up barroom ballad is about camaraderie. It serves both to underscore your group-ness, and to help a newcomer (if he drinks like a good sport) feel like one of the gang.

Why should foreigners have all the fun? How about some drinking songs for us! It's time, fellow wine-snobs, to put some *joie de vivre* into that solemn tasting group of yours.

And why not start with these excerpts from *The American Wine Geek's Songbook:*

Ninety-two, ninety-four!
Only buy the wines that score
No thinking! (chug)
Ninety-six, ninety-eight!
Only wines the critics rate
Safe drinking! (chug)

Here's to the bottles from days of old
Here's to the ones we have still
Drink 'em or hold, drink 'em or hold?
Too late - they've gone over the hill
Over the hill, boys, over the hill, my futures are over the hill!
Drink 'em or hold, drink 'em or hold?
The question is bugging me still

Will Mondavi ever finish turning ninety?
Alas, me lads, it's graver than you fear
A publicist on java
Drinking Gavi in her cava
Told Mondavi to turn ninety every year!

Raise up high the auction paddle
Hey Napa Napa and a wham bam bash
Bid-up your own lot, then skedaddle
Stick it to the bidder with the cash
Bidder from Cremona
Bidder from Pamplona
Bidder from Sonoma with a blond bim-bo
Millionaires stampeding like a herd of cattle
Stick it to the sucker with the dough

Here's a toast to you, me mates
Tip your glass with me
Any glass will do, me mates
As long as it's hand-blown, lead crystal with 12 3/8-ounce
bowl, tapering to a narrow, cut edge, suitable for Grüner
Veltliner, Jurançon Sec, and Riesling (Smaragd), but definitely
not for Pinot Blanc or Riesling (Kabinett).

1. Red, red wine
Messed up my life
Lost me my kids
Cost me my wife
Drink and the devil
Are the road to strife
Red, red wine.

2. Doctor, doctor
What can be done?
It ain't the red wine
That's killing you, son.
Look at the studies
Every last one
Says drink red wine

3. Red, red wine
Good for the heart
Shores up the prostate
And it makes you smart
Grabs free radicals
And rips them apart
Good red wine

4. Red, red wine
Fixed up my life
Lost my spare tire
To the surgeon's knife
Got a Maseratti
And a trophy wife
Thanks, red wine!

Glass Half-Full

Stranded in a dry house

Brothers and sisters, I have a confession to make: I drink wine. Some people find that disturbing. If you spend much time with this type you learn that not only is it hard to enjoy wine when you're the only one drinking, but it brings on the sort of irrational guilt that makes you sneak by the bell-ringing Santa, even though you gave generously at the office.

I have great admiration for the discipline of recovered alcoholics. But when they say, "Go ahead and have wine, it won't bother me," I can't shake the feeling that flaunting my forbidden fruit around them is a cruel tease. Wouldn't a good friend refrain?

I once dated a serious gourmet, newly sober, who put on a spread for me at his house with silver, candles, six amazing courses, and the perfect wine to match each one. In half bottles, just for me. How uncomfortable is that? You mellow out, get a little uninhibited, while he remains completely sober. Now that

267

I think about it, perhaps that was the plan. Well, for the record, it worked.

Some eschew wine for their religion; others just don't cotton to it. A slew of Americans consider wine a fancy-schmancy treat for special occasions. They do not understand the concept of daily wine. It's as though you insisted on confetti and a swing-band at every meal.

Their abstemiousness skews their sense of capacity. My friends in the wine business often put back a bottle a day. They are not drunks. They are acclimated. To say nothing of the training benefits of drinking at 5,280 feet, the elevation of my mile-high city.

Dinner at a dry house is agonizing. Your thimble-sized glass is filled once, before the bottle runs aground at the other end of table. As a guest, you can't pour yourself more, assuming there even *is* more. I've known trained wine professionals, when houseguests, to hide a bottle in the bedroom and swig it on the sly, making them exactly the person of low moral character the hosts take them for.

The rumbling undercurrent of disapproval boils down to this unspoken accusation: *You've got a problem. Do you really NEED that glass of wine?* And you begin to wonder; do I? So then it's time to roll out the Europeans, as in—*they* drink wine with every meal! Always have. Always will. Except they always won't, because younger Europeans are moving, on the one hand to martinis, and on the other to zero-tolerance.

You turn, then, to science. Studies show that drinking wine is healthy! And yet when the doctor asks about your weekly consumption, how many of you—show of hands, please—fudge a little, for fear they'll take away your children and ship you to Betty Ford?

What's a wine-lover to do? "I just ignore it," says a colleague, "I don't care what they think; I drink my wine."

"If they make me feel that uncomfortable drinking, I stop seeing those people," says another.

Neither solution works for me. I'm too thin-skinned to ignore the buzz and I'm not about to ditch my friends. But it's hardly wine if you don't share it.

The worst is when someone really cares, and tries to get you to spend an evening without wine so they can "get to know the real you." A sort of test. I've got news for those people: the *real me* drinks wine with dinner every night! And once in a while (gasp!) with lunch, too.

Who's the Greatest!?

Triumphant comeback for wine snob

New York, NY: A gruesome swirling accident, followed by multiple carpal tunnel and pinkie surgeries couldn't keep him down. Competing for the first time in fifteen months, Ainsworth Teasdale trounced last year's champion Gerald "The Jereboamator" DeWitt to claim the title of International Wine Bore of the Year.

"I'm exuberant," said Teasdale, "with notes of unrestrained glee and a hint of *schadenfreude!*"

DeWitt, the two-to-one favorite, wasn't taking the loss lightly. "That poseur doesn't know his bunghole from *botrytis!*" he complained.

But Teasdale's volley of tendentious boasts, clocked at an amazing two-per-minute, proved too much for the defending champ.

"Trockenbeerenauslese!" a triumphant Teasdale shouted to the 15,000-some fans packed into the stadium. "No one volatizes the esters like me!"

"'I'm exuberant,' said Teasdale, 'with notes of unrestrained glee and a hint of schadenfreude!'"

Teasdale's pompous style never deserted him. In the Restaurant event, always one of his best, he persuaded a sommelier to decant seven wines that didn't need it, a world record, and then launched into his trademark, "That reminds me of the time..." the famous twenty-six-minute monologue about his vertical of Le Pin, that has stadium crowds all over the country on their feet doing the Funky Corkscrew.

The second event, In-Home Boredom, had the crowd gasping when DeWitt served a record forty-seven wines at a dinner party for four, but Teasdale maintained the lead by passing around digital photos of his cellar, newly refinished in East Indian zebrawood and Cuban granite, with a micro-hydraulic counter-mounted cork extractor and a walk-in thermidor for wineglasses. "Humidity, temperature and pressure are crucial to keeping my crystal tuned to the correct frequencies," he intoned.

DeWitt made a strong showing in the Description phase with "Nuances of bruised finberry wreathed in ripe Asian moonfruit," but was bested by Teasdale's shockingly concise: "Hawaiian volcanic-ash-tinged notes of duck's breath."

"I don't know what happened out there," said a dazed DeWitt. "I was off my rhythm, I guess. I was feeling honest, down to earth. In fact, I was kind of enjoying the wine," he concluded to a stunned press.

Teasdale, 48, has been a regular on the wine-bore circuit for more than four years. At the Trophy Hunter's Invitational in 2001 he brought six sommeliers to their knees when he sent back a bottle of 1923 Yquem, a feat still unmatched.

Then came the accident, at the time thought to be career-ending. For a while Teasdale kept up a brave façade, endorsing Cartier's line of platinum *tastevins*, and starring in the popular reality series "Who Wants to Stuff a Cork in this Guy?"

But then he seemed to lose focus. There was the cult-wine scandal, where it was discovered Teasdale's name was on only seven allocation lists, far short of the twenty-four he had claimed. Competing on the amateur circuit brought him a string of heartbreaking losses culminating in the Barolo Bore-Off. It looked like Ainsworth Teasdale was finished. Rumors had him sipping White Zinfandel at a scrapbooking party.

But somehow he rallied. Back in form, thanks to a grueling training regiment of foie gras, ossetra caviar and Andalusian cracked pepper, the Tease looked stronger than ever.

And he proved it by arriving at the arena with a Bordeaux glass bigger than his head.

"Damn it, that's MY annoying affectation," DeWitt complained.

Teasdale responded by whipping out an even bigger Burgundy glass and shouting, "Hey, Jerry! Swirl this!" The infraction cost him two penalties, but the crowd loved it.

Moments later, though, DeWitt was back in the game, racing through a 100-page wine list directly to the first-growths in less than a minute, a move he premiered at the 2001 Alsace Open.

Event number four, Name Dropping, was the turning point. This had long been thought the weak point of Teasdale's snob appeal, but his social-climbing skills surfaced today, as he bored the crowd with interminable anecdotes involving Piero, Angelo, two Michels and three Bobs.

As the crowd erupted in thunderous a snoring ovation, it was clearly all over but the spitting.

Teasdale easily sustained his lead through Supercilious Lip Curling and Dismissive Gestures, to come away with the upset victory.

"You dream about this as a kid," said Teasdale, his horn-rimmed glasses misting up.

Where does he get his mental toughness? "I just keep my eye on the cork and take it one sip at a time."

Asked if he had a message for his fans, the new World Champion looked squarely into the cameras and said, "White. It's the new Red."

About the Author

Jennifer Rosen was a 2003 finalist for the Jacob's Creek International Best Drinks Writer award. Her wine column appears weekly in the *Rocky Mountain News* and *Denver Post* in Colorado, and a network of other papers across the nation. It also flies around the world to close to 10,000 subscribers of her Internet newsletter.

She's a regular contributor to *Wine Enthusiast, The Beverage Network, Drinks Magazine* and the *New Zealand Winepress,* and also writes for *The Independence Institute, Long Island Wine Gazette* and *The Wine Club Newsletter.*

Jennifer partnered with Microsoft to develop software and a series of interactive blind tasting seminars for CEOs around the country. Other clients for her seminars include *Beaulieu Vineyards,* the *Colorado Symphony Orchestra,* the *Denver Art Museum, Immedient Corporation* and *Toastmasters International.* She's heard nationally on syndicated radio show *Pierre Wolfe's Food & Wine,* and is a regular monthly guest on the *Mike Rosen Show.*

An Advanced Sommelier with the International Wine Guild, she lives in Denver and travels frequently to wine regions around the world, where she speaks French and Italian, stutters Spanish and German and has begun destroying the Arabic language. She is certified as a ski instructor, horse trainer and handwriting analyst. Jennifer works off the job perks with belly dancing and trapeze.

You can subscribe to her weekly column at: www.vinchotzi.com

Index

Give the Gift of

WAITER, THERE'S A HORSE IN MY WINE

to Your Friends and Colleagues

CHECK YOUR LEADING BOOKSTORE OR ORDER HERE

❑ **YES**, I want _____ copies of *Waiter, There's a Horse in My Wine* at $14.95 each, plus $4.95 shipping per book (Colorado residents please add $1.07 sales tax per book). Canadian orders must be accompanied by a postal money order in U.S. funds. Allow 15 days for delivery.

❑ **YES**, I am interested in having Jennifer Rosen speak or give a seminar to my company, association, school, or organization. Please send information.

My check or money order for $_____ is enclosed.

Please charge my ❑ Visa ❑ MasterCard ❑ Discover ❑ American Express

Name_____

Organization_____

Address_____

City/State/Zip _____

Phone_____ E-mail_____

Card #_____

Exp. Date_____Signature_____

Please make your check payable and return to:

Dauphin Press

245 S Garfield St

Denver, CO 80209

Fax or email your credit card order to:

603-925-3755 or Dauphin1@vinchotzi.com